THE BIG BOOK OF AWESOME ACTIVITIES

Kidsbooks®

3535 West Peterson Avenue
Chicago, IL 60659

Printed in China
061401026JZ

***Visit us at* www.kidsbooks.com**

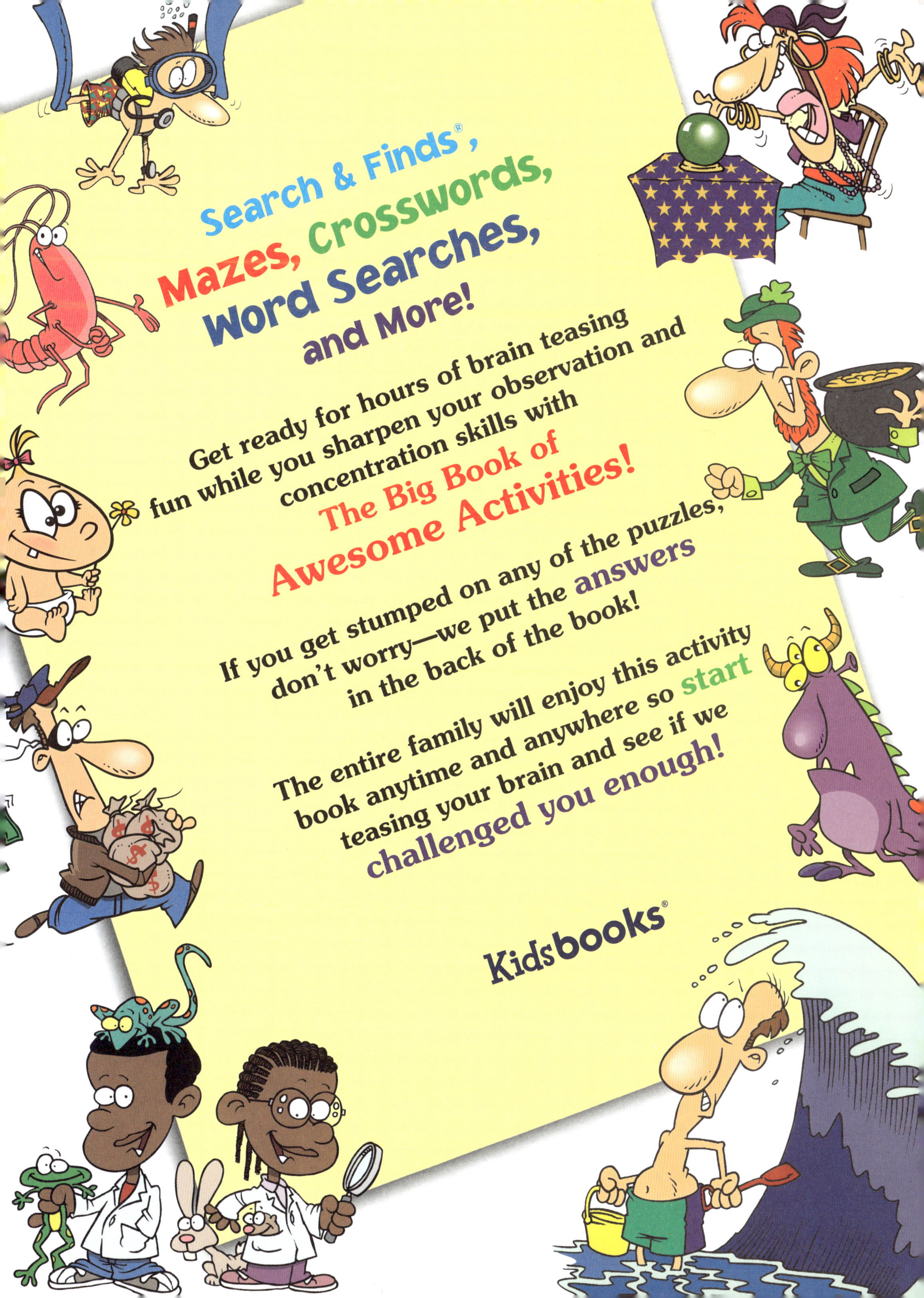
Search & Finds®,
Mazes, Crosswords,
Word Searches,
and More!
Get ready for hours of brain teasing fun while you sharpen your observation and concentration skills with
The Big Book of Awesome Activities!
If you get stumped on any of the puzzles, don't worry—we put the answers in the back of the book!
The entire family will enjoy this activity book anytime and anywhere so start teasing your brain and see if we challenged you enough!
Kidsbooks®

Rhyme Time

Find a word that rhymes with each word listed below, using the clues in the parentheses. Then read down the column in blue to answer the question:

"What rhymes with 'orange'?"

1) SEA (body part) ____________

2) HOWL (garden tool) ____________

3) FIRST (explode) ____________

4) HARP (pointy) ____________

5) HEIGHT (chew) ____________

6) FROWN (funny guy) ____________

7) SPONGE (fall) ____________

Answers on Page 180

In Action

Use the clues below to complete this crossword puzzle about actions.

ACROSS

1 On skates, bikes, or scooters
4 Go high in the air
5 Up a tree or mountain
7 To stroll

DOWN

2 Big jump
3 Don't leave the water _____
5 Babies, before walking
6 Birds and planes and kites

1 2 3 4 5 6 7

Answers on Page 180

Decode-a-Riddle

Write the letter that comes **THREE LETTERS BEFORE** each letter shown below to decode and solve this riddle.

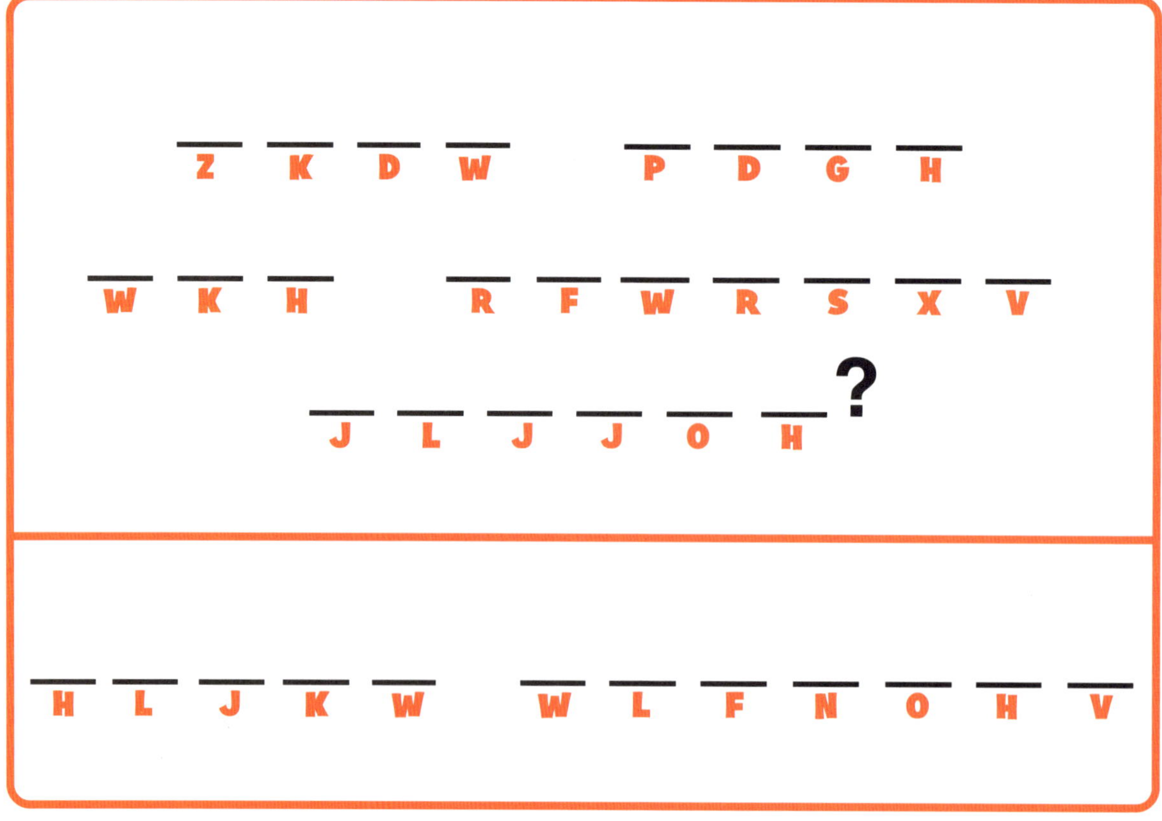

Answers on Page 180

Double Popsicles

Can you find the two pictures that are exactly alike?

Answers on Page 180

Fascination

Can you make **25** words or more from this word?

FASCINATION

Answers on Page 181

Musical Mayhem

The show is about to start—and the musicians can't find their instruments! Help the musical trio find their instruments by following the path from **Start** to **Finish**.

Answers on Page 181

Trucks

Search, find, and circle these **10** things.

CHICKENS (3)
FOX
DUMBBELL
TOTEM POLE
MUMMY
MAGNET
MICE (2)
TEAPOT
LIGHTHOUSE
ROBOT

Answers on Page 181

Poetic Puzzle

Solve this rebus puzzle to learn the name of a great American poet.

Answers on Page 181

Lazy Sunday

Find **two sets of two objects** that rhyme with each other.

Answers on Page 182

State Capitals

Put the capital that goes with each state in the crossword below.

Answers on Page 182

Bust-a-Beat

Find **10** differences between the picture on the left and the one on the right.

Answers on Page 182

Word Scramble

Unscramble each of these words using the clues.

(Likes to fly)

_ _ _ _

(Summer month)

_ _ _ _

(Number game)

_ _ _ _

(Tells time)

_ _ _ _ _

Answers on Page 183

Find these words that have to do with fishing in this word search.
Look up, down, backward, forward, and diagonally.

CAST
ROD
BAIT
CATFISH
WORM 
CLEARWATER
LAKE
BOAT
FLY
REEL

U	O	S	D	B	U	V	W	N	E	W	D	V	M
Z	B	R	W	K	G	C	T	E	W	T	P	H	M
X	C	F	E	C	G	A	Q	A	Y	T	R	C	M
X	I	A	R	E	F	S	U	S	O	R	D	C	I
G	T	E	T	C	L	T	N	G	X	B	P	G	X
F	M	A	D	F	M	X	K	M	J	R	L	Y	J
Y	J	K	B	P	I	H	H	K	R	A	G	W	N
W	T	I	R	L	B	S	L	P	K	O	U	A	M
F	O	P	U	A	E	C	H	E	Z	S	W	D	S
D	Z	A	I	T	C	F	H	Y	E	I	G	C	O
G	M	T	T	G	L	B	X	G	K	J	L	Y	T
Q	V	Z	U	Y	V	D	O	R	U	H	L	C	N
D	D	R	E	T	A	W	R	A	E	L	C	S	Q
B	J	Y	G	W	D	V	C	P	Y	I	A	X	N

Answers on Page 183

Where Am I?

Use the clues below to complete this crossword puzzle.

ACROSS	DOWN
3 Circling	1 Not indoors
5 Hidden in back of	2 Enter the building
6 In the middle	4 Above
7 Beneath	6 Next to

Answers on Page 183

Decode-a-Message

Use the code key below to find a message that is considered an artistic intrument

A=3	D=9	N=10	R=2
B=11	E=1	O=8	Y=4
C=6	L=5	P=7	

__ __ __   __ __ __ __ __ __

2 1 9   6 2 3 4 8 10

Answers on Page 183

Word Game

Look at the pictures below. Figure out what phrase uses these words and fill it in on the lines below.

__ __ __ __ __ __ __

__ __ __ __ __ __ __ __ __.

Answers on Page 184

Celebration

Can you make **25** words or more from the following word?

CELEBRATION

Answers on Page 184

Sudoku

Fill in the empty squares so that each row, column, and square box contains the numbers **1-9** only once.

4		3	6		8		2	9
		1	5				4	
9	8	7			2	1	6	5
3	9		8				7	
		6	9	2	3	5	8	
1			4	7	5		3	6
			7			6		4
8	1	4						
6	7	9	1	3	4			8

Answers on Page 184

Use the pictures below to complete this crossword puzzle.

across

1

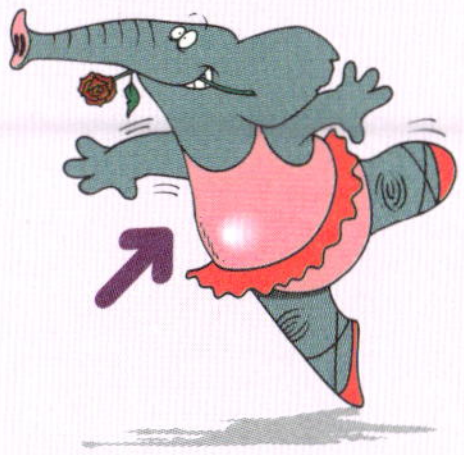

2

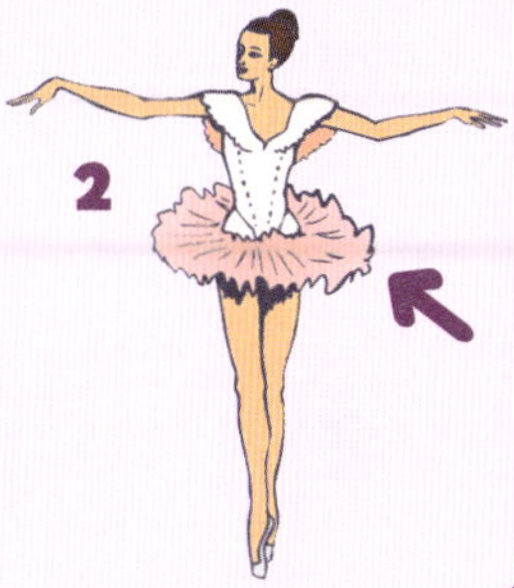

DOWN

3

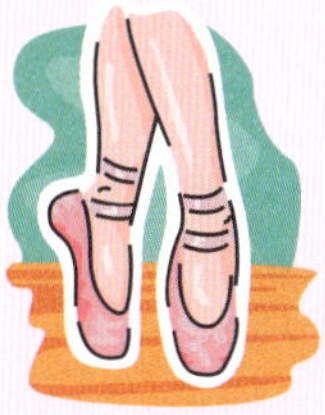

4

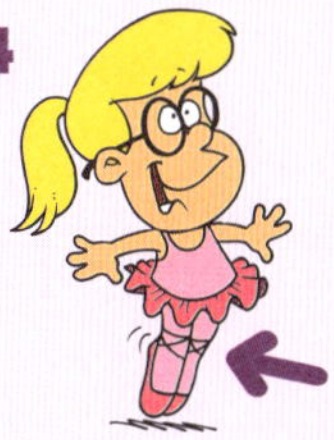

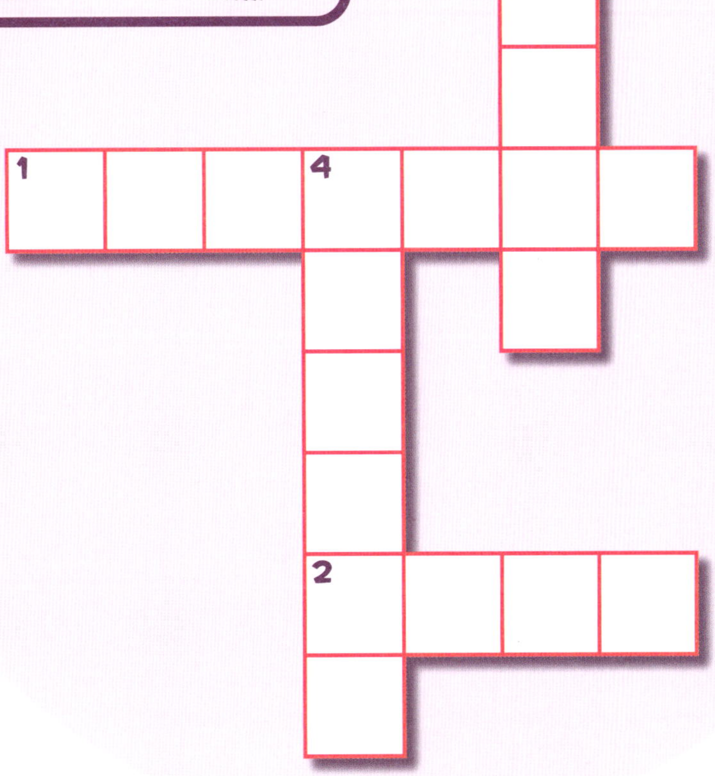

1

4

3

2

Answers on Page 184

Slippery Stuff

Solve this rebus puzzle to find something fruity that you shouldn't eat.

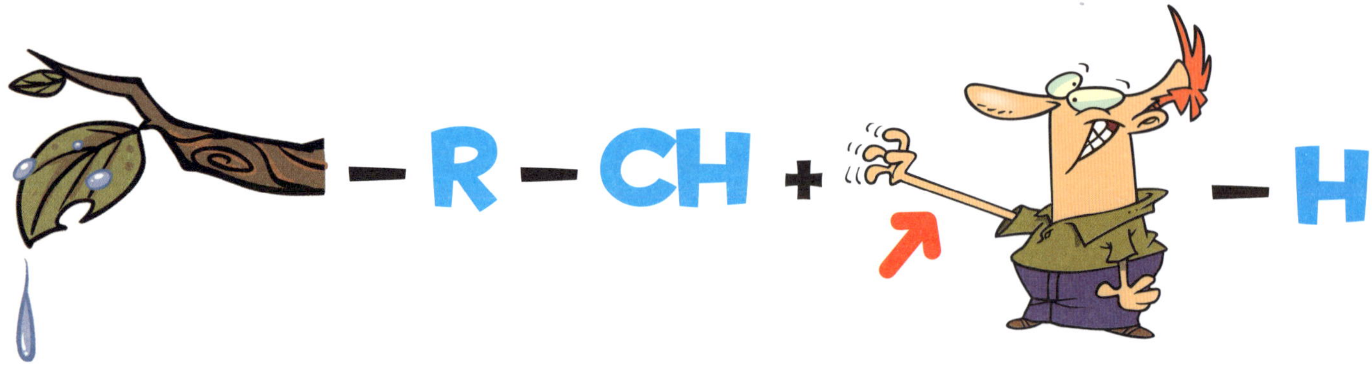

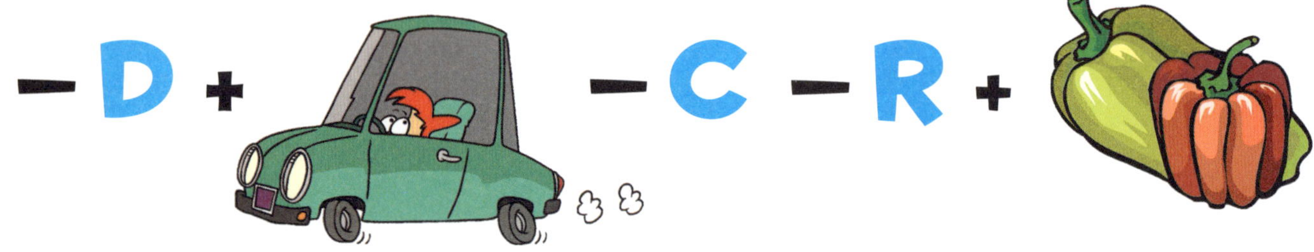

– PPERS + – E

Answers on Page 185

Creative Puzzle

Look at the pictures below. Figure out what phrase uses these words and fill it in on the lines below.

___ ___ ___ ___,

___ ___ ___ ___ ___.

Answers on Page 185

Take a Trip

Use the clues below to complete this crossword puzzle.

ACROSS

1 You need these for the plane or train
5 Things to remember your trip by
6 Where to eat on a trip
8 Reference for info
9 Pack this up with clothes
10 Book in advance

DOWN

2 Snap those pictures
3 Mail these to your friends
4 Best seats on the plane
7 Leads you in a new place

Answers on Page 185

Fill in the empty squares so that each row, column, and square box contains the numbers **1-9** only once.

3					4			6
2		7						9
8								
			7	2				
					3	1		8
				5		6	3	
		8			5			
	2				8	9	1	
9	1		6			7		

Answers on Page 185

Strike Out

Search, find, and circle these **10** things.

BANANA PEELS (3)	**DUCK**	**YO-YO**
BASKETBALL	**MOUSE**	**BONE**
CLOWN	**ROLLER SKATES**	**APPLE CORE**
	HAMBURGER	

Answers on Page 186

Word Scramble

Unscramble each of these words using the clues.

ILDAGFRUE
(Water rescue)

_ _ _ _ _ _ _ _ _

IMEETTSLO
(Christmas leaves hung in doorway)

_ _ _ _ _ _ _ _ _

SGNATYM
(Athlete)

_ _ _ _ _ _ _

NUUAMT
(Season)

_ _ _ _ _ _

AUMERSETPKR
(Food source)

_ _ _ _ _ _ _ _ _ _ _

EAMDMRI
(Fishy person)

_ _ _ _ _ _ _

AAGORKON
(Animal)

_ _ _ _ _ _ _ _

ALANSAG
(Food)

_ _ _ _ _ _ _

Answers on Page 186

Tennis

Find these words that have to do with tennis in this word search.
Look up, down, backward, forward, and diagonally.

Answers on Page 186

Lucky Number Three

Going from **Start** to **Finish**, choose the path made up of the number **3** only.

Start

3	2	4	4	2
3	1	8	7	6
3	3	1	5	8
2	3	1	6	9
7	3	6	8	7
9	3	3	3	3

Finish

Answers on Page 186

Rescue Vehicles

Based on the **problem** below, determine the appropriate rescue vehicle. Use the clues below to complete this crossword puzzle.

ACROSS
1 Broken leg
2 House fire
3 Search and rescue

DOWN
4 Burglar
5 Sea distress

Answers on Page 187

Decode-a-Riddle

Use the code key below to find something that you would cook in your home.

A=5	E=6	I=2	M=3	S=4
C=11	G=13	K=7	N=12	U=14
D=1	H=9	L=8	P=10	

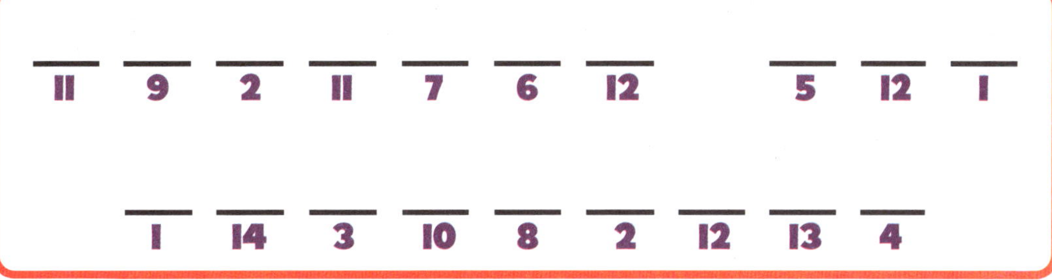

Answers on Page 187

Double Octopuses

Can you find the two pictures that are exactly alike?

Answers on Page 187

A Balanced Diet

Can you make **25** words or more from the following phrase?

A BALANCED DIET

Answers on Page 187

Odd Birthday Maze

Guide this boy to the birthday cake by choosing the path made of **ODD** numbers only. You can only go **UP**, **DOWN**, and **ACROSS**—not diagonally.

Start

5	7	10	16	4	12
11	2	13	8	11	23
3	14	7	21	8	3
21	1	3	25	2	5
6	20	18	15	8	4
2	12	6	5	7	9
4	19	3	17	6	2
10	1	12	22	28	14
2	21	5	13	10	16
6	17	4	19	12	9
3	5	8	27	11	5

Finish

Answers on Page 188

Holiday Time

Put the color of each holiday in the crossword below.

Answers on Page 188

Super Singer

Solve this rebus puzzle to find someone talented and famous.

Answers on Page 188

Hardware Store

Find **two sets of two objects** that rhyme with each other.

Answers on Page 188

Pumpkin Harvest

Find **10** differences between the picture on the left and the one on the right.

Answers on Page 189

U.S. Cities

Put the city of each attraction in the crossword puzzle below.

ACROSS

2 The White House
3 Hollywood
5 Mile High City
7 Golden Gate Bridge
8 Paul Revere

DOWN

1 Liberty Bell
4 Sears Tower
6 Empire State Building

Answers on Page 189

Word Scramble

Unscramble each of these words using the clues.

REFLWO
(Blooming plant)

_ _ _ _ _ _

LDSALA
(Texas city)

_ _ _ _ _ _

GLUJEN
(Land of thick vegetation)

_ _ _ _ _ _

HTEGI
(Not seven or nine)

_ _ _ _ _

LETBLA
(Type of dance)

_ _ _ _ _ _

TROAC
(Pretending professional)

_ _ _ _ _

Answers on Page 189

Tools

Find these types of tools in this word search. Look up, down, backward, forward, and diagonally.

S	S	D	F	M	R	U	I	Z	H	T	R	P	Y
T	C	I	R	E	P	A	R	C	S	W	A	S	Z
T	T	R	I	B	Y	R	M	I	I	F	Z	K	E
E	B	X	E	D	W	H	I	O	X	X	J	Q	D
L	J	A	T	W	J	R	H	A	M	M	E	R	B
L	L	H	X	H	D	S	E	L	A	N	Z	V	J
A	R	J	F	E	A	R	L	N	O	M	V	X	T
M	Y	M	O	N	V	I	I	U	C	B	J	M	L
W	O	U	D	R	R	Q	G	V	X	H	C	M	V
S	Z	E	H	D	Q	M	Y	H	E	U	P	W	R
P	R	I	V	R	P	S	H	W	T	R	K	W	T
K	D	S	I	D	C	E	H	T	F	K	Z	Q	F
S	F	G	E	G	D	U	E	K	Y	Y	X	X	M
D	D	U	X	A	C	R	D	Y	M	J	B	A	Y

Answers on Page 190

Running Errands

This woman has one more errand to run, but her daughter keeps trying to tell her something. What's on the little girl's mind? Cross out the word "mom" wherever it appears to find out what she is trying to say.

IMOMMOMNMOMEMOMEMOM
DMOMMOMTOMOMGOMOM
MOMTOMOMTMOMHMOMMOM
EMOMPMOMOMOMTMOMTMOMY!

Answers on Page 190

Summer Fun

Search, find, and circle these **10** things.

BOOK
SHOVEL
SAILOR
KITE
ALLIGATOR
COWBOY
ELEPHANT
MERMAID
BONE
MARSHMALLOW

Answers on Page 190

Decode-a-Riddle

Use the code key below to decode and solve this riddle.

1=A	8=H	15=O	22=V
2=B	9=I	16=P	23=W
3=C	10=J	17=Q	24=X
4=D	11=K	18=R	25=Y
5=E	12=L	19=S	26=Z
6=F	13=M	20=T	
7=G	14=N	21=U	

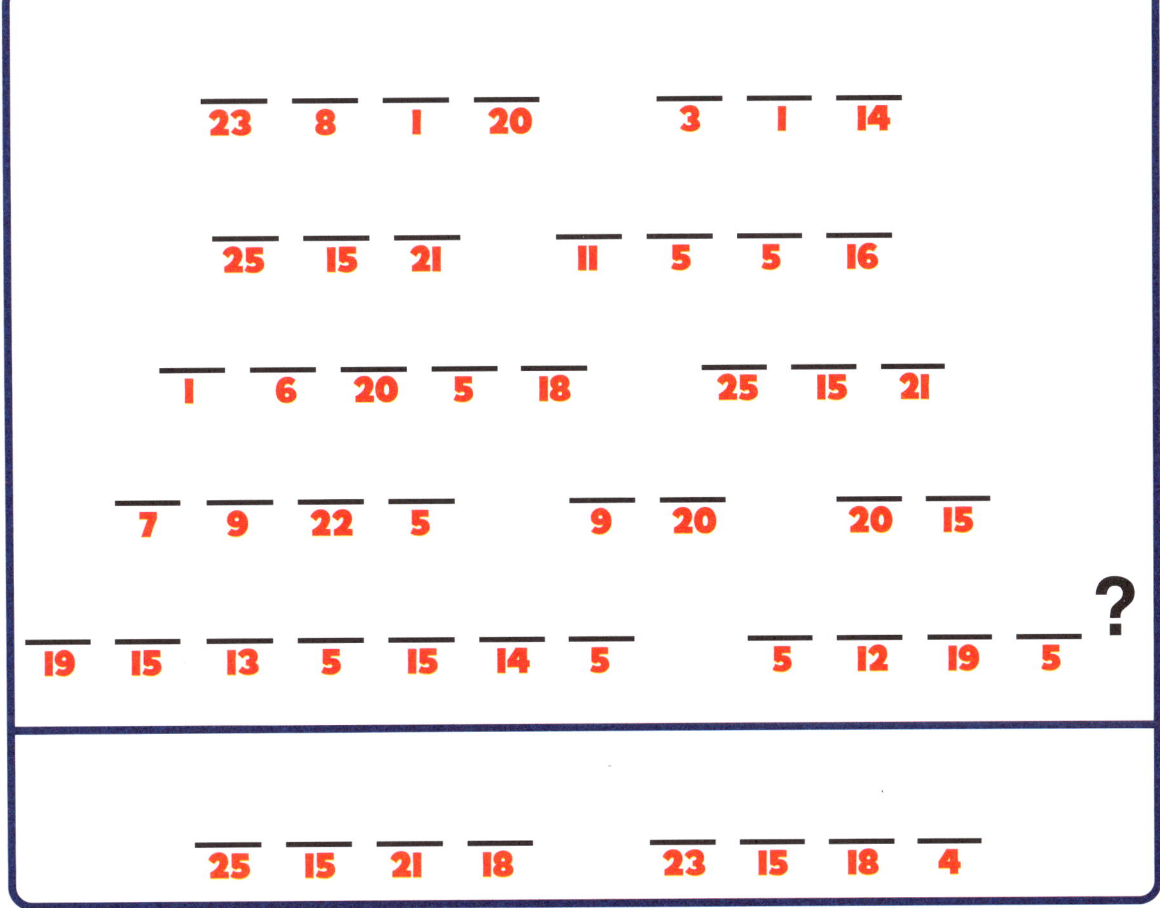

Answers on Page 190

Double Bananas

Can you find the two pictures that are exactly alike?

Answers on Page 191

Can you make **25** words or more from the following word?

AGRICULTURE

Answers on Page 191

Shark Maze

Help the leopard shark get back to the sea floor. Make sure to avoid the tiger shark, which might just make the leopard shark its dinner!

Answers on Page 191

Animals

Use the pictures below to complete this crossword puzzle.

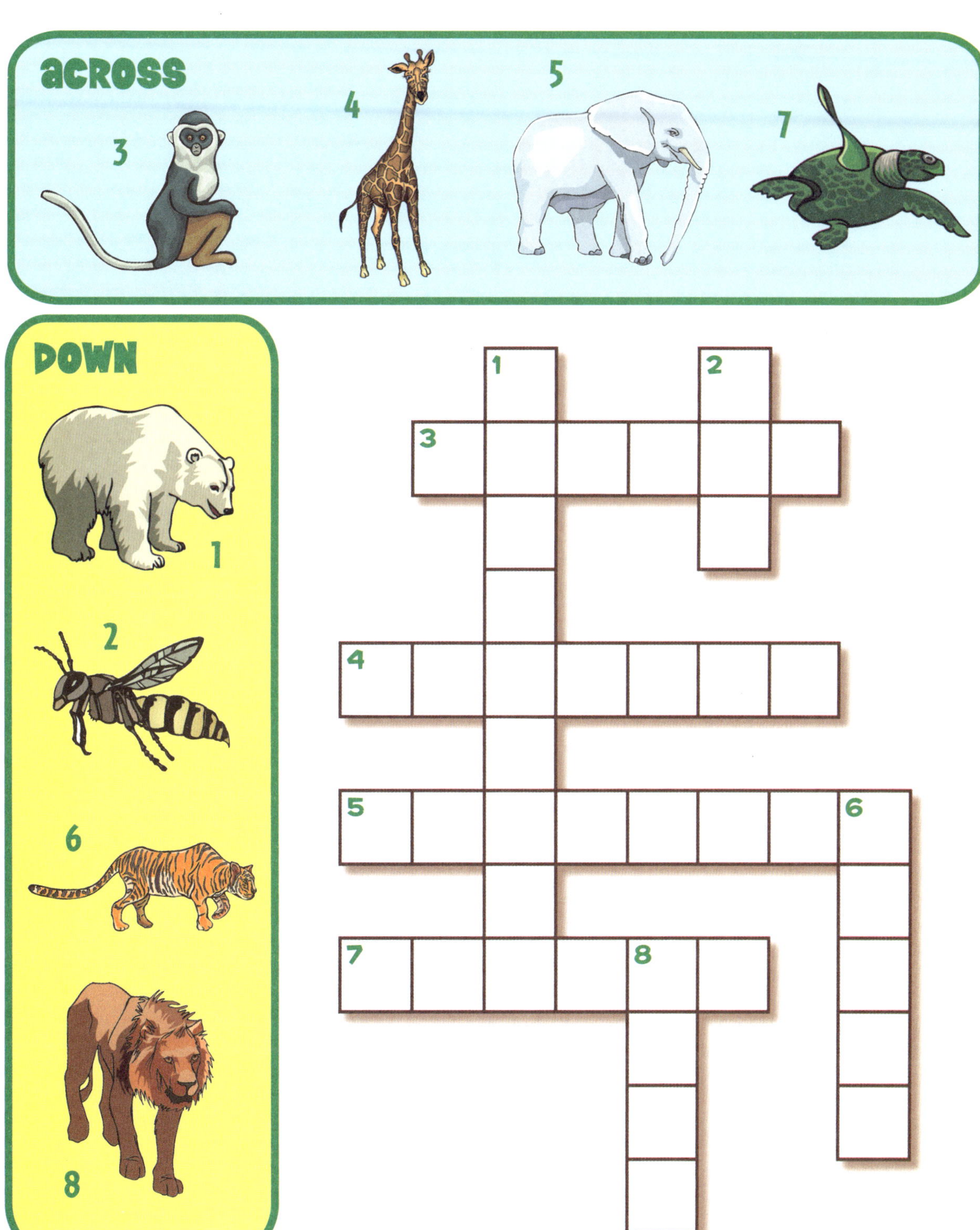

Answers on Page 191

Camera Parts

Find these camera parts in the word search.
Look up, down, backward, forward, and diagonally.

FILM	BATTERIES
LENS	STRAP
SHUTTER	BODY
MOUNT	LEVER
FLASH	VIEWFINDER

S	B	P	R	R	O	F	P	A	H	Z	Z	H
N	H	A	D	C	O	I	U	D	X	W	O	P
X	R	O	T	F	O	L	F	G	E	L	S	I
T	P	E	L	T	K	M	A	K	R	P	H	M
X	P	E	D	Z	E	Z	M	E	L	S	X	Q
S	N	I	D	N	R	R	T	X	A	A	I	M
S	O	C	W	K	I	T	I	L	A	W	R	O
Y	D	V	L	R	U	F	F	E	Y	V	E	U
X	D	S	V	H	U	X	W	H	S	M	V	N
Y	X	O	S	P	P	Q	Y	E	U	B	E	T
B	A	Q	B	M	C	R	L	G	I	A	L	O
M	V	T	F	E	Q	Z	S	T	G	V	O	H
C	L	K	O	S	T	R	A	P	O	W	D	Q

Answers on Page 192

Team Time

Use the clues below to complete this crossword puzzle.

ACROSS

3 Oakland baseball team
6 Atlanta hockey team
8 Cleveland basketball team
9 St. Louis baseball team
10 LA baseball team

DOWN

1 New York football team
2 Toronto hockey team
4 Dallas football team
5 Boston basketball team
7 New England football team

Answers on Page 192

Wonderful Wizards

Search, find, and circle these **10** things.

ALIEN	**FLYING PIG**	**SOCCER BALL**
CANDY CANE	**ICE-CREAM CONE**	**SPIDERS (6)**
COW	**OWLS (7)**	**TENNIS RACKET**
	SANTA CLAUS	

Answers on Page 192

Sudoku

Fill in the empty squares so that each row, column, and square box contains the numbers **1-9** only once.

4		9	3	7		8	5	6
		8	4					3
	7	3			8	2		4
2		6		5		3		
7		1	2	4	3	5		8
5		4		8		9		2
3				9			8	5
8		7	6			4		
9	4	5		1	2	6		7

Answers on Page 192

Sticky Stuff

Solve this rebus puzzle to find the name of a delicious lunch.

Answers on Page 193

Word Scramble

Unscramble each of these words using the clues.

TRENASTUAR
(Eating place)

_ _ _ _ _ _ _ _ _ _

CTYDNRIIAO
(Word describer)

_ _ _ _ _ _ _ _ _ _

RHCYISMTE
(Class subject)

_ _ _ _ _ _ _ _ _

RELIOPCHET
(Aircraft)

_ _ _ _ _ _ _ _ _ _

RPNEAAIL
(Sky coach)

_ _ _ _ _ _ _ _

LABLSBAE
(Throwing game)

_ _ _ _ _ _ _ _

SMULCE
(Under your skin)

_ _ _ _ _ _

OOIUYSLLQ
(Singly speaking)

_ _ _ _ _ _ _ _ _

Answers on Page 193

Types of Dance

Find these types of dance in this word search. Look up, down, backward, forward, and diagonally.

BALLROOM
BALLET
FOLK
TANGO
MODERN
JAZZ
POLKA
TAP
SALSA
SQUARE

E Q M F E P Y D Q E G J R Q
B R Y S O T S J Y D Q U U Q
J V A L J X U A F B Q F K M
R N K U E C Y J L R G M D Q
Z A E E Q C H B K S R C Q N
T V J X I S T E L L A B G L
C A N U C K Y S S R O M R O
X R P R Q O C J W J O F W E
I X R P E X W N P O L O L L
Y N O B U D Q B R J U G T X
A D A H K S O L U V P N A N
O C G L T D L M Z Z A J N J
Y K K N P A S N N O V R G A
C G L D B D E H I W G E O J

Answers on Page 193

Word Game

Look at the letters in the box below. Figure out what phrase about singing includes "**GIG**" and fill it in the lines below.

__ __   __ __ __ __ __ __ __

__ __ __ __

Answers on Page 193

Use the clues below to complete this crossword puzzle.

ACROSS
4 Fresh and natural
6 Eat it at your birthday party
7 Frozen sweet treat
9 Thick and chocolaty
10 Liquid ice-cream drink

DOWN
1 Baked chocolate squares
2 Apple, pumpkin, chocolate cream
3 Lots in a box
5 Soft and sweet, chocolate or butterscotch
8 Drink it with cookies

Answers on Page 194

Decode-a-Message

Use the code key below to find a message that has to do with dreaming.

A=2	H=16	O=13	T=3
C=12	I=7	P=5	U=8
D=4	M=15	R=6	W=14
E=10	N=9	S=11	Y=1

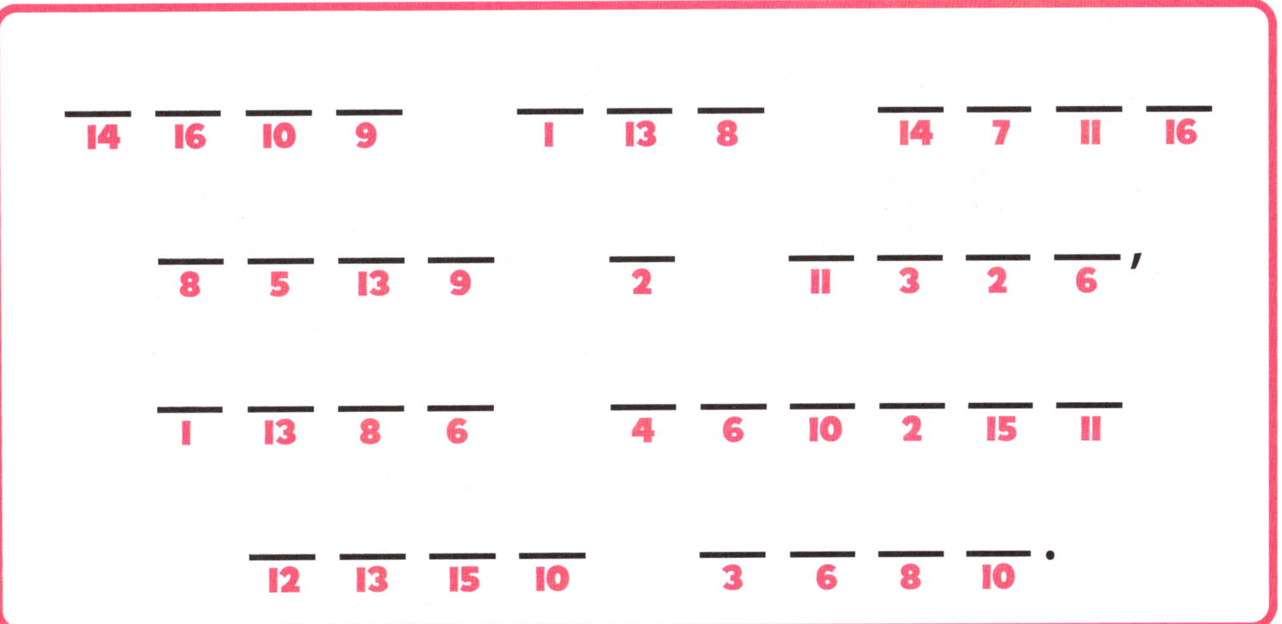

Answers on Page 194

Double Ladybugs

Can you find the two pictures that are exactly alike?

Answers on Page 194

Engagement

Can you make **25** words or more from the following word?

ENGAGEMENT

Answers on Page 194

Even Bear Maze

Guide this bear to the honeycomb by choosing the correct path made of **EVEN** numbers only.

Answers on Page 195

Vehicle Sounds

Put the sounds associated with each picture in the crossword puzzle below.

Answers on Page 195

Mythical Animal

Solve this rebus puzzle to find the name of a mythical animal.

—A— MENT

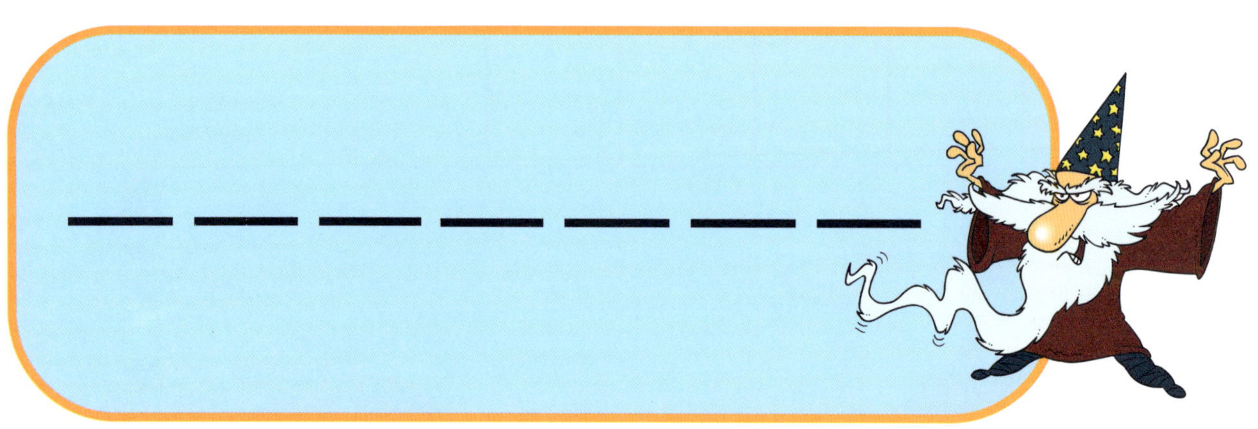

Answers on Page 195

Double Dinosaurs

Can you find the two pictures that are exactly alike?

Answers on Page 195

Safari Trip

Find **10** differences between the picture on the left and the one on the right.

Answers on Page 196

Airplanes

Search, find, and circle these **10** things.

APPLE	BIRDS' NEST	TOAST
BASEBALL	CLOWNS (5)	TOOTHBRUSH
BEACH BALL	FISHBOWL	ZEBRA
	ROBOT	

Answers on Page 196

Word Scramble

Unscramble each of these words using the clues.

TNCFORON
(Face up against)

_ _ _ _ _ _ _ _

LEGRAYL
(Place where art is shown)

_ _ _ _ _ _ _

TANGINMAIOI
(Creative thinking)

_ _ _ _ _ _ _ _ _ _ _

CATINTRATO
(Appeal, pull)

_ _ _ _ _ _ _ _ _ _

CIVDEENE
(Proof)

_ _ _ _ _ _ _ _

DUNHATE
(Filled with ghosts)

_ _ _ _ _ _ _

GAGUNALE
(Word of a country)

_ _ _ _ _ _ _ _

JASMAAP
(What you wear to bed)

_ _ _ _ _ _ _

Answers on Page 196

Fish

Find these types of fish in this word search. Look up, down, backward, forward, and diagonally.

Shark	Barracuda
Eel	Goldfish
Salmon	Haddock
Bass	Flounder
Sunfish	Anglerfish

I	P	L	A	N	E	U	O	R	Q	J	G	F	Q
F	L	D	L	A	B	R	N	R	B	O	H	K	C
F	H	W	T	Q	Y	K	C	F	L	U	S	F	S
N	I	Q	E	E	L	K	W	D	R	A	I	H	S
Y	K	R	A	H	S	I	F	F	D	V	F	H	A
R	S	S	H	H	Z	I	X	U	O	H	R	K	B
C	L	A	C	S	S	Z	C	N	G	O	E	C	C
K	Y	L	Z	H	I	A	K	D	N	U	L	O	E
Y	A	M	U	S	R	F	Y	S	D	D	G	D	Q
U	J	O	H	R	L	S	N	Q	A	J	N	D	Y
D	U	N	A	C	S	S	X	U	Z	V	A	A	F
X	H	B	Y	X	E	U	Y	R	S	O	A	H	K
J	F	L	O	U	N	D	E	R	S	C	A	C	H
L	H	T	Q	S	K	V	H	A	S	G	L	D	V

Answers on Page 197

Fill in the empty squares so that each row, column, and square box contains the numbers **1-9** only once.

8		5			6	2	4	
1	7		5		4			8
	6	3	1	2		9	5	
2		1	4			8		
	3			5	7		2	
		6			9	5		4
	1	8	3		5			2
		7		8		6		3
3		9	6	4			8	

Answers on Page 197

Use the clues below to complete this crossword puzzle.

ACROSS	DOWN
4 Clear and simple	1 Brewed from a bag
5 Grind and brew	2 From fruit
6 Sweet and bubbly	3 Made with lemons
8 To gulp down	7 Good with chocolate

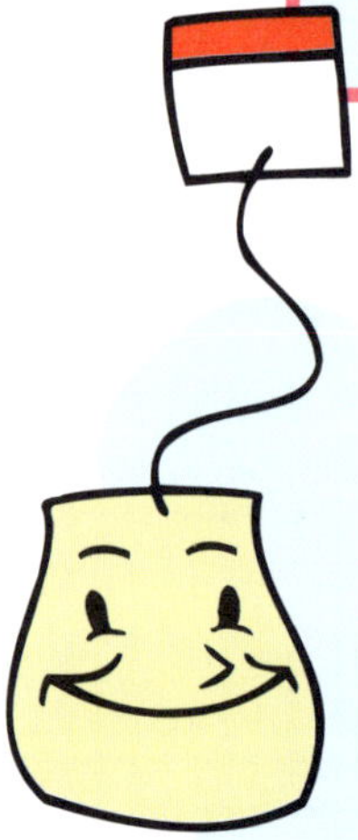

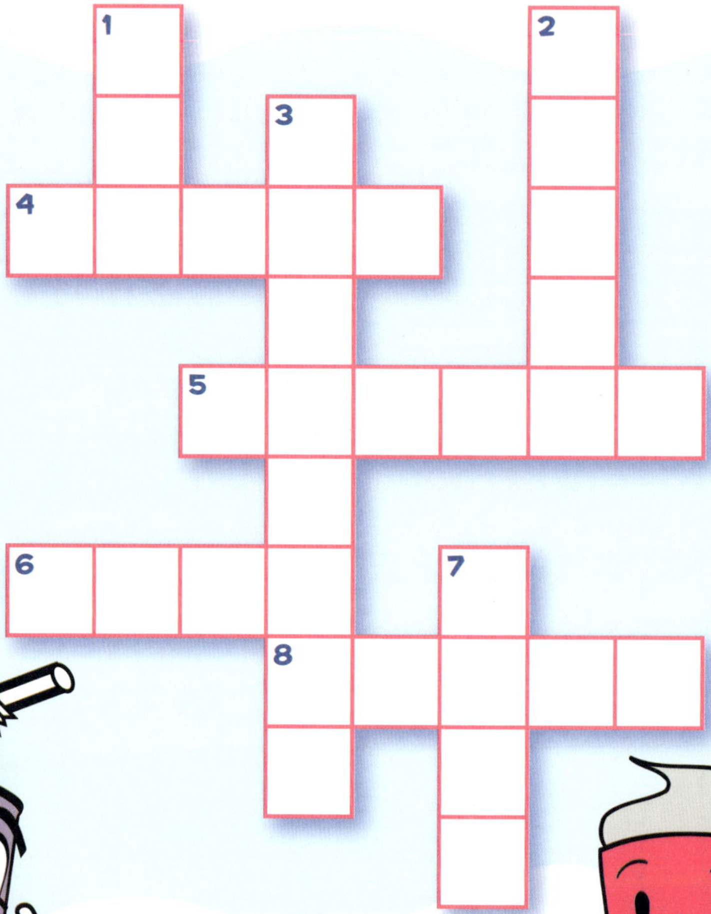

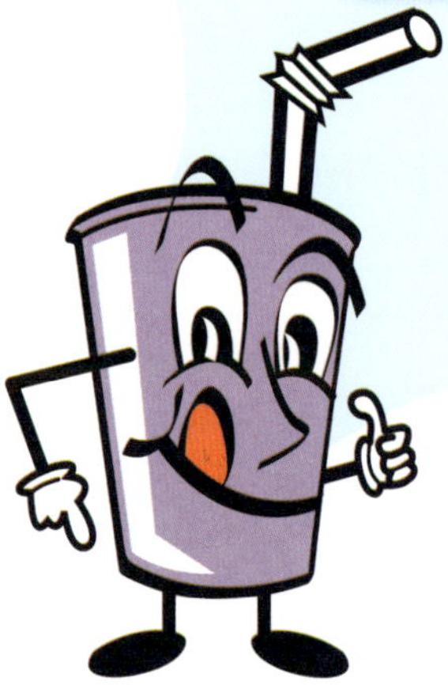

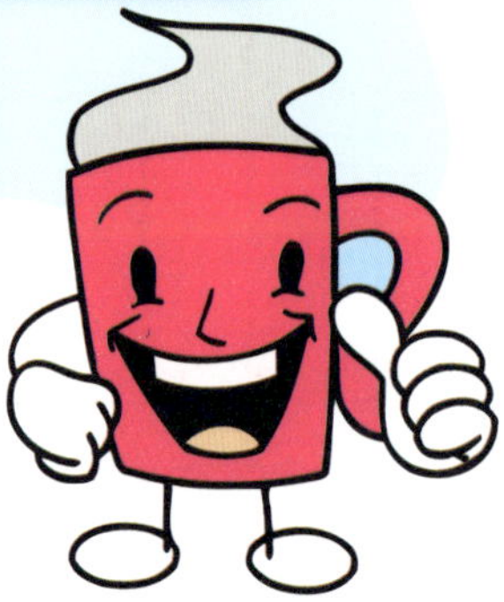

Answers on Page 197

Decode-a-Message

Use the code key below to find a message that has to do with a wintry day.

A=4 H=3 T=2
C=1 O=5

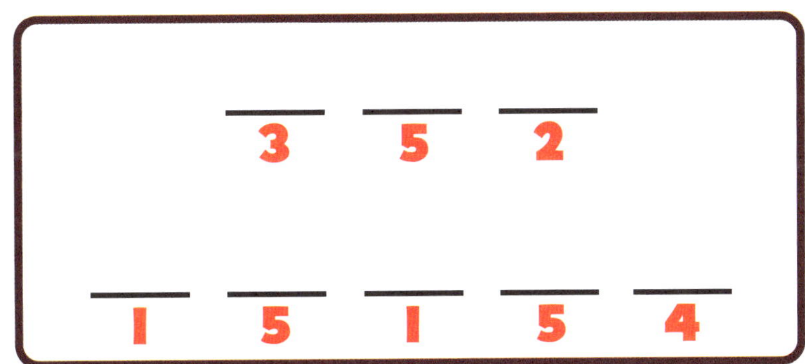

Answers on Page 197

Space Adventures

Follow the path from **Start** to **Finish** to help the lunar rover find its way to the space station.

Answers on Page 198

Can you make **25** words or more from the following word?

BURGLARIZE

Answers on Page 198

Lucky Number Two

Going from **Start** to **Finish**, choose the path made up of the number **2** only.

2	2	3	7	3
5	2	2	5	5
6	9	2	8	8
7	7	2	7	9
8	5	2	2	7
9	4	3	2	2

Answers on Page 198

State Capitals

Put the capital that goes with each state in the crossword puzzle below.

Answers on Page 198

Wet Adventure

Solve this rebus puzzle to find a neat place to explore.

— S +  — E

+  — RA +  —

S — ET +  — L

Answers on Page 199

Opposites Attract

List the opposite of each word in the spaces below. Then read down the column to learn the opposite of **OUTSIDE**.

1) DARK ____________

2) OLD ____________

3) ENEMIES ____________

4) SMALL ____________

5) SHALLOW ____________

6) DRY ____________

Answers on Page 199

Bull's Eye

Follow the path from **Start** to **Finish** to guide the dart thrower to the bull's eye.

Answers on Page 199

Fill in the empty squares so that each row, column, and square box contains the numbers **1-9** only once.

						2		
8		3	2				9	
	4		9	7		6		
			7		9			1
	9	6	3		1	7	8	
3			5		6			
		5		3	4		1	
	6				2	4		3
		8						

Answers on Page 199

Carnival Fun

Search, find, and circle these **10** things.

BASEBALL GLOVE
BOWLING BALL
COTTON CANDY
FLAG
LION
ROBOT
JACK-O'-LANTERN
SKATEBOARDS (2)
UNICYCLE
FRANKENSTEIN

Answers on Page 200

Word Scramble

Unscramble each of these words using the clues.

TEGILINNS
(Paying attention to)

_ _ _ _ _ _ _ _ _

YERVNOEE
(All the people)

_ _ _ _ _ _ _ _

RATHEFES
(On a bird)

_ _ _ _ _ _ _ _

GIPVIRLEE
(Advantage, special treatment)

_ _ _ _ _ _ _ _ _

GALMENGI
(Shining)

_ _ _ _ _ _ _ _

SELNERLETS
(Persistant, not stopping)

_ _ _ _ _ _ _ _ _ _

PIWRESH
(Speak softly)

_ _ _ _ _ _ _

KRADYABC
(Behind the house)

_ _ _ _ _ _ _ _

Answers on Page 200

Bicycle Ride

Find these words that have to do with a bicycle in this word search.
Look up, down, backward, forward, and diagonally.

Q	H	S	Y	D	S	J	N	E	R	I	T	I	M
R	B	H	H	V	E	U	C	P	F	S	U	C	E
A	E	O	D	U	S	E	B	D	U	K	J	W	H
J	L	E	G	H	C	E	H	Z	L	P	R	S	G
U	L	S	G	A	I	E	V	E	P	S	L	X	Z
R	B	X	M	K	N	O	F	O	L	W	J	M	L
A	P	M	U	P	C	B	A	M	L	M	F	U	V
B	D	D	V	F	L	Y	C	K	C	G	E	I	C
E	E	K	B	X	I	F	B	Y	D	M	H	T	J
L	N	L	F	M	N	J	Y	E	D	E	C	H	H
D	K	H	C	I	E	B	E	A	Z	P	W	F	X
N	P	F	A	G	Z	I	C	P	T	D	K	D	N
A	B	H	B	P	B	F	Q	Z	L	O	C	K	E
H	C	H	V	U	K	O	I	R	Z	J	P	P	L

Answers on Page 200

Let's Build

Unscramble these construction vehicles on the blanks below and then place them in the crossword puzzle.

Answers on Page 200

Game Time

Use the clues below to complete this crossword puzzle.

ACROSS

1 Kings and queens
5 Toss a ball back and forth
8 Hand off the baton
9 Card game with bids
10 Three water birds
11 Two hands, no tackling

DOWN

2 Find the missing item
3 Ready or not, here I come
4 Spin the rope, jump
5 Jump my piece
6 You're it!
7 Small glass balls

Answers on Page 201

Lunchtime

Use the code key below to find a something that has to do with a lunchbreak.

A=8	F=16	K=9	R=10
B=14	G=1	M=15	S=6
C=11	H=5	N=7	T=12
E=4	I=2	O=3	W=13

___ ___ ___ ___   ___ ___ ___ ___ ___ ___ ___,
1 3 7 4   16 2 6 5 2 7 1

___ ___ ___ ___   ___ ___ ___ ___ ___ ___ ___ ___.
14 8 11 9   12 3 15 3 10 10 3 13

Answers on Page 201

Double Kites

Can you find the two pictures that are exactly alike?

Answers on Page 201

Anatomical

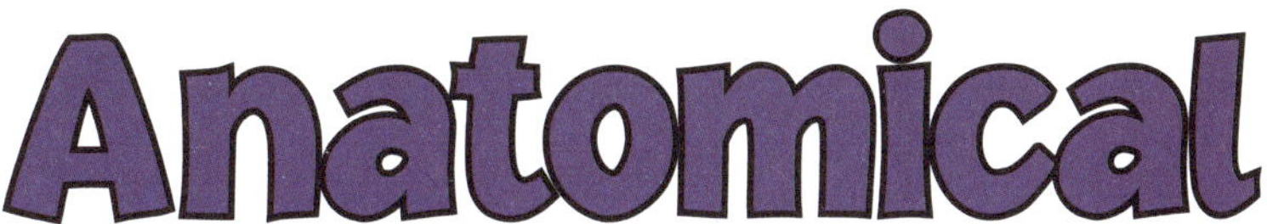

Can you make **25** words or more from the following word?

ANATOMICAL

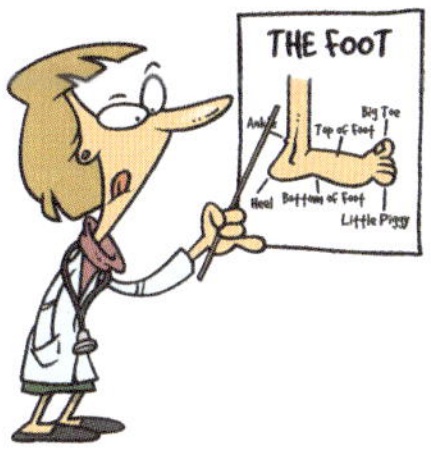

Answers on Page 201

Odd House Maze

Guide this woman back to her house by choosing the correct path made of **ODD** numbers only. You can only go **UP**, **DOWN**, and **ACROSS**—not diagonally.

Start

1	6	4	8	2	1			
2	1	3	12	1	4			
10	4	17	3	13	21			
8	12	3	2	9	12	3	9	11
4	16	9	10	11	8	9	2	3
12	7	5	8	9	1	5	4	7
9	2	9	3	10	3	4	1	10
1	3	10	15	7	19	5	3	7
		8	4	17	4	2	9	8
		5	6	12	13	10	5	5
		5	9	15	7	3	17	2

Finish

Answers on Page 202

Under the Sea

Use the pictures below to complete this crossword puzzle.

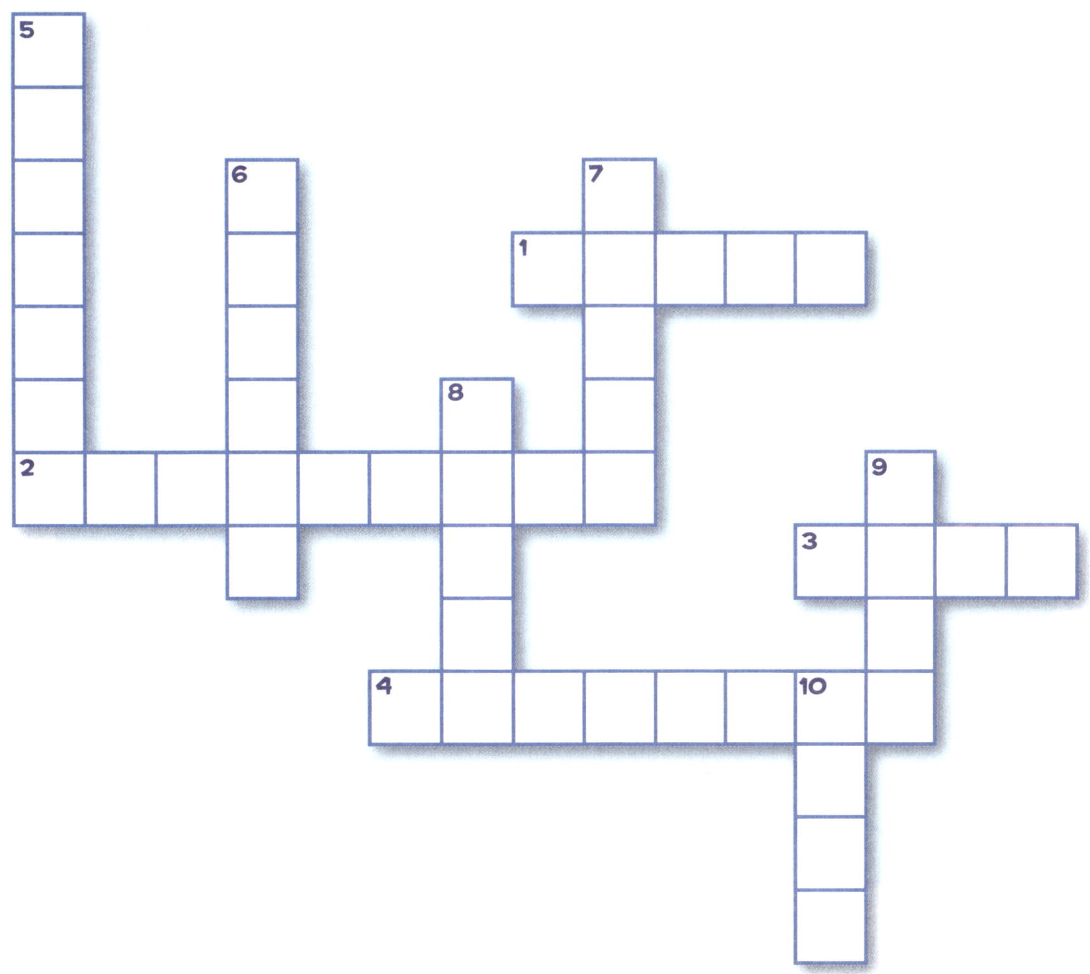

Answers on Page 202

On the Go

Solve this rebus puzzle to find something you need when you travel.

Answers on Page 202

Sudoku

Fill in the empty squares so that each row, column, and square box contains the numbers 1-9 only once.

2		9	5	8		7		6
6							5	
		5	6	4		9		2
	5	3	2			4		
9				5	4	6	1	
4	6		8	3	9			7
	9			7	2	3		
3	2	6		9				
5	7			6	8		9	1

Answers on Page 202

Ice Hockey Game

Find **10** differences between the picture on the left and the one on the right.

Answers on Page 203

Traveling Circus

Search, find, and circle these **10** things.

BALLOONS (14)	FIRE HYDRANT	PARTY HAT
BANJO	HAMBURGERS (2)	PENGUIN
CRICKET	MOUSE	TURTLES (4)
	NECKTIE (3)	

Answers on Page 203

Word Scramble

Unscramble each of these words using the clues.

ACPEH
(Juicy summer fruit)
_ _ _ _ _

SHUP
(To shove)
_ _ _ _

POTS
(Halt, cease)
_ _ _ _

PLHE
(Assist)
_ _ _ _

ROYRW
(To fret, be concerned)
_ _ _ _ _

ARHI
(It's on your head)
_ _ _ _

GTHIL
(Bright, glowing bulb)
_ _ _ _ _

UHTTR
(Honestly)
_ _ _ _ _

Answers on Page 203

Car Parts

Find these car parts in this word search. Look up, down, backward, forward, and diagonally.

Tailgate
Bumper
Tire
Dashboard
Engine
Brakes
Horn
Grille
Hubcap
Exhaust pipe

H	W	O	B	D	K	E	N	O	E	N	N	O	K
R	L	B	F	U	E	R	R	R	U	B	O	B	Y
V	R	D	L	K	M	L	C	I	O	D	N	C	J
B	Z	E	O	E	T	P	L	U	T	H	M	Q	E
X	M	F	L	W	M	G	E	B	X	T	T	F	X
J	K	H	T	L	P	U	R	R	O	A	V	K	H
Q	O	E	U	A	I	A	Y	U	I	W	V	W	A
K	N	V	Q	B	K	R	Q	L	F	N	U	K	U
V	R	R	Q	E	C	G	G	L	Q	R	V	A	S
L	U	H	S	A	D	A	N	I	M	B	Z	W	T
I	U	V	G	E	T	C	P	C	X	Z	F	Y	P
F	N	B	Z	E	D	O	E	N	I	G	N	E	I
S	P	J	R	J	Y	Q	T	M	V	G	Z	M	P
S	R	D	A	S	H	B	O	A	R	D	Z	J	E

Answers on Page 204

Land the Plane

Think like a pilot and help guide the plane to the landing strip.
It's your job to follow the path from **Start** to **Finish**.
Prepare for landing!

Answers on Page 204

Authors

Write these famous authors' first names in the blanks below and then complete this crossword puzzle.

ACROSS
1 ___ Christian Anderson
2 ___ Kipling
3 ___ Dickens
4 ___ Shelley
5 ___ Austen

DOWN
1 ___ Melville
2 ___ Waldo Emerson
5 ___ London
6 ___ Carroll
7 ___ Hodgson Burnett

Answers on Page 204

Decode-a-Riddle

Use the code key below to find something that has to do with a little bambino.

A=4	I=8	S=2
B=1	M=9	T=5
E=6	O=3	Y=7

___ ___ ___ ___
1 4 1 7

___ ___ ___ ___ ___ ___ ___
1 3 5 5 3 9 2

Answers on Page 204

Double Aliens

Can you find the two pictures that are exactly alike?

Answers on Page 205

Influenza

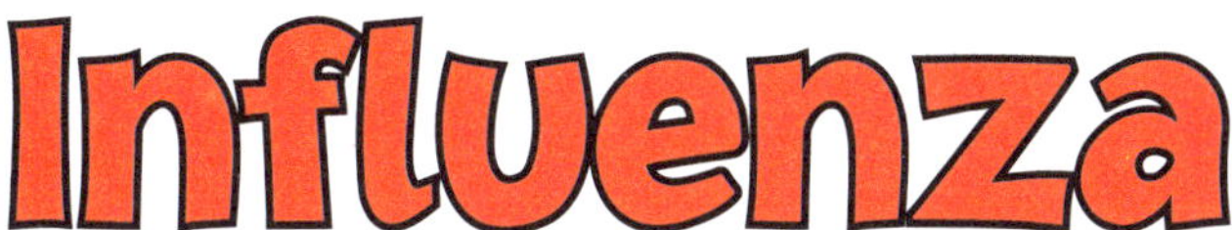

Can you make **25** words or more from the following word?

INFLUENZA

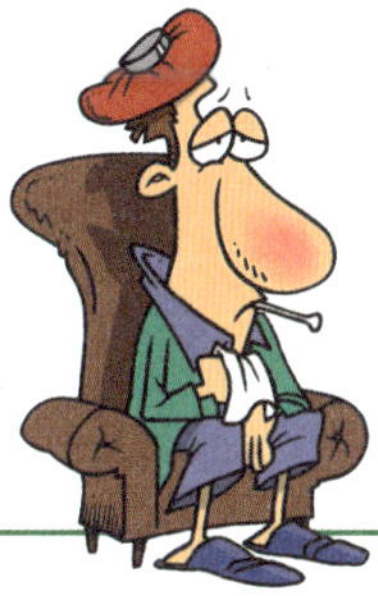

Answers on Page 205

Shopping Time

Guide this man through this maze to the cashier by putting **1** to **36** in the correct order. You can only go **UP**, **DOWN**, and **ACROSS**—not diagonally.

Start

6	5	4	3	2	1			
7	6	5	4	5	2			
8	9	10	5	12	3			
9	8	7	6	11	4			
20	21	22	7	10	5			
19	24	23	8	9	6			
18	19	12	11	10	7			
17	20	21	22	11	8			
16	15	14	13	12	9	10	11	12
17	18	19	20	21	22	23	24	13
20	19	36	35	26	25	24	15	14
			34	33	32	25	26	27
			33	34	35	26	35	28
			32	35	28	27	30	29
			31	30	29	32	31	30
			32	33	34	35	32	31

Finish

Answers on Page 205

I'm Hungry

Use the pictures below to complete this crossword puzzle.

Answers on Page 205

Dangerous Weather

Solve this rebus puzzle to find out a sign of dangerous weather.

+ AST + — I — G +

— C — R + O + —

GON + R + — ETY + G

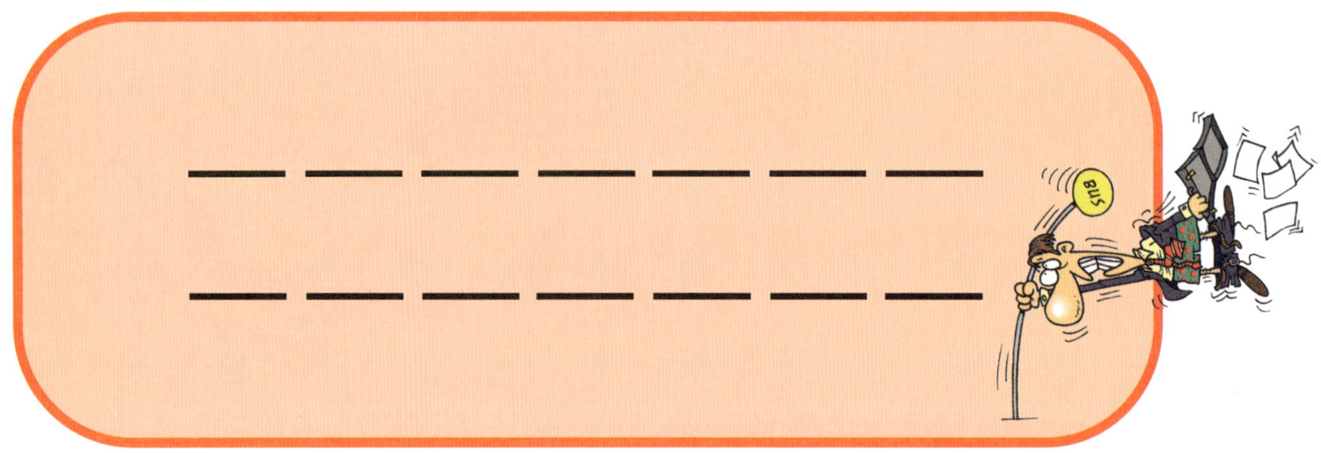

Answers on Page 206

Class Schedule

Put the school subjects of each topic in the crossword puzzle below.

ACROSS

1 Latitude/ Longitude

2 Expressionism

3 Pythagorean Theorem

DOWN

4 Sonnet

5 War of 1812

6 Empirical Charts

Answers on Page 206

Beach Time

Find these things that have to do with the beach in the word search. Look up, down, backword, forward, and diagonally.

Lotion
Sand
Ocean
Chair
Umbrella
Swimsuit
Waves
Shovel
Swimming
Surfing

W	A	G	V	U	M	B	R	E	L	L	A	W	A
O	R	N	A	Q	H	F	Y	T	S	S	U	M	Y
V	S	I	M	P	I	K	L	W	C	U	V	D	B
O	H	M	J	B	J	Q	I	F	E	M	R	J	U
Y	O	M	Y	I	A	M	Q	N	L	K	U	X	H
R	V	I	P	A	S	R	B	O	A	L	D	U	C
I	E	W	V	U	K	Y	T	T	B	E	M	C	P
A	L	S	I	Q	W	I	R	J	R	B	C	X	B
H	B	T	Z	X	O	A	N	D	P	B	Q	O	J
C	P	O	G	N	Q	R	V	X	N	P	T	W	R
B	X	R	G	K	M	P	L	E	K	A	T	Y	G
L	C	P	F	N	A	M	A	Q	S	U	S	Q	K
S	U	R	F	I	N	G	G	J	S	I	B	B	G
X	K	P	A	S	H	W	O	T	G	A	A	O	X

Answers on Page 206

Sudoku

Fill in the empty squares so that each row, column, and square box contains the numbers **1-9** only once.

7				8		3		
	9		4		1			8
8		2		7				
3			8		9		7	2
	8			2		6	3	4
4						8		
		4			8	2		
						5		
6				5		4		3

Answers on Page 206

Dino Paradise

Search, find, and circle these **10** things.

BABY CARRIAGE	CAKE	POPCORN
BASKETBALL	CHEESE	SLIDE
BERET	FEATHER	VOLLEYBALLS (2)
	PAIL	

Answers on Page 207

Word Scramble

Unscramble each of these words using the clues.

VDOE
(Bird of peace)

_ _ _ _

HWOS
(Performance)

_ _ _ _

HCSOK
(Surprise, stun)

_ _ _ _ _

LADE
(Hand out cards)

_ _ _ _

KACP
(Put into a suitcase)

_ _ _ _

KRWO
(Do a job)

_ _ _ _

PLIF
(Turn over)

_ _ _ _

IJNO
(Become part of a club or team)

_ _ _ _

Answers on Page 207

Types of Birds

Find these types of birds in this word search. Look up, down, backward, forward, and diagonally.

Mockingbird	Wren
Heron	Sparrow
Hummingbird	Woodpecker
Shorebird	Warbler
Bluebird	Duck

P	J	W	R	E	N	D	J	S	J	H	B	M	C
G	H	J	I	Q	Q	O	H	G	U	L	H	O	R
U	L	C	K	P	N	O	B	M	U	N	E	C	L
A	L	C	C	U	R	R	M	E	U	C	R	K	O
T	W	M	X	E	B	I	B	K	G	C	O	I	G
M	I	O	B	K	N	I	Z	C	H	L	N	N	E
R	S	I	O	G	R	Q	M	U	J	B	N	G	N
I	R	P	B	D	X	C	S	D	R	K	T	B	C
D	M	I	A	A	P	J	R	S	A	Q	C	I	X
P	R	U	C	R	B	E	U	L	C	R	X	R	X
D	T	B	G	J	R	S	C	U	F	O	B	D	T
Y	W	X	R	D	A	O	R	K	D	T	C	J	L
Y	O	R	E	L	Q	J	W	M	E	S	O	X	D
N	G	M	R	E	L	B	R	A	W	R	T	V	K

Answers on Page 207

Militaristic

Unscramble these things that have to do with the military on the blanks below and then place them in this crossword puzzle.

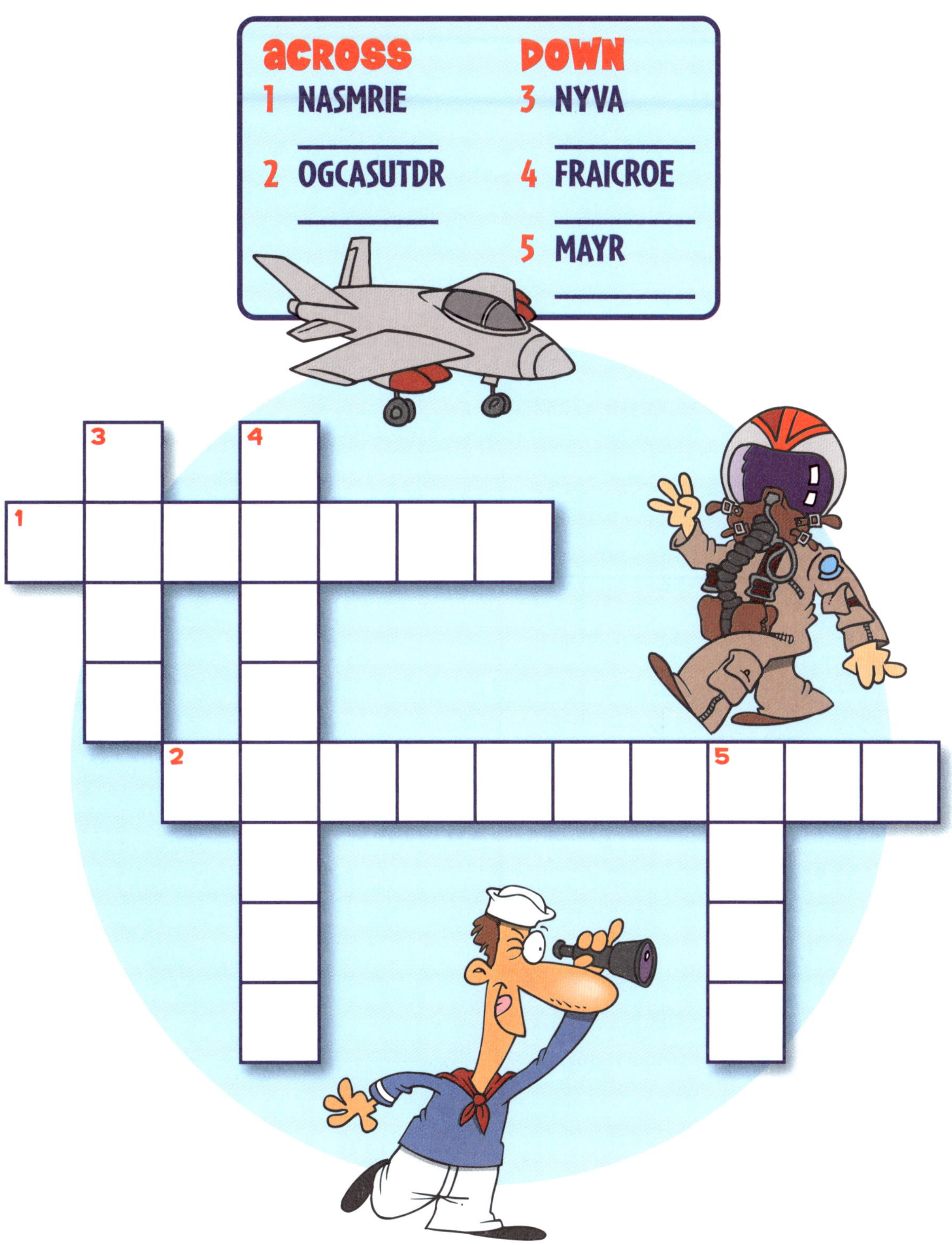

Answers on Page 207

Musical Instruments

Use the clues below to complete this crossword puzzle.

ACROSS

4 Long, silver woodwind instrument

5 Woodwind instrument that sounds like a duck

6 Jazz instrument with a double reed

DOWN

1 Biggest baritone brass instrument

2 Second largest, upright orchestra instrument

3 Highest-pitched band instrument

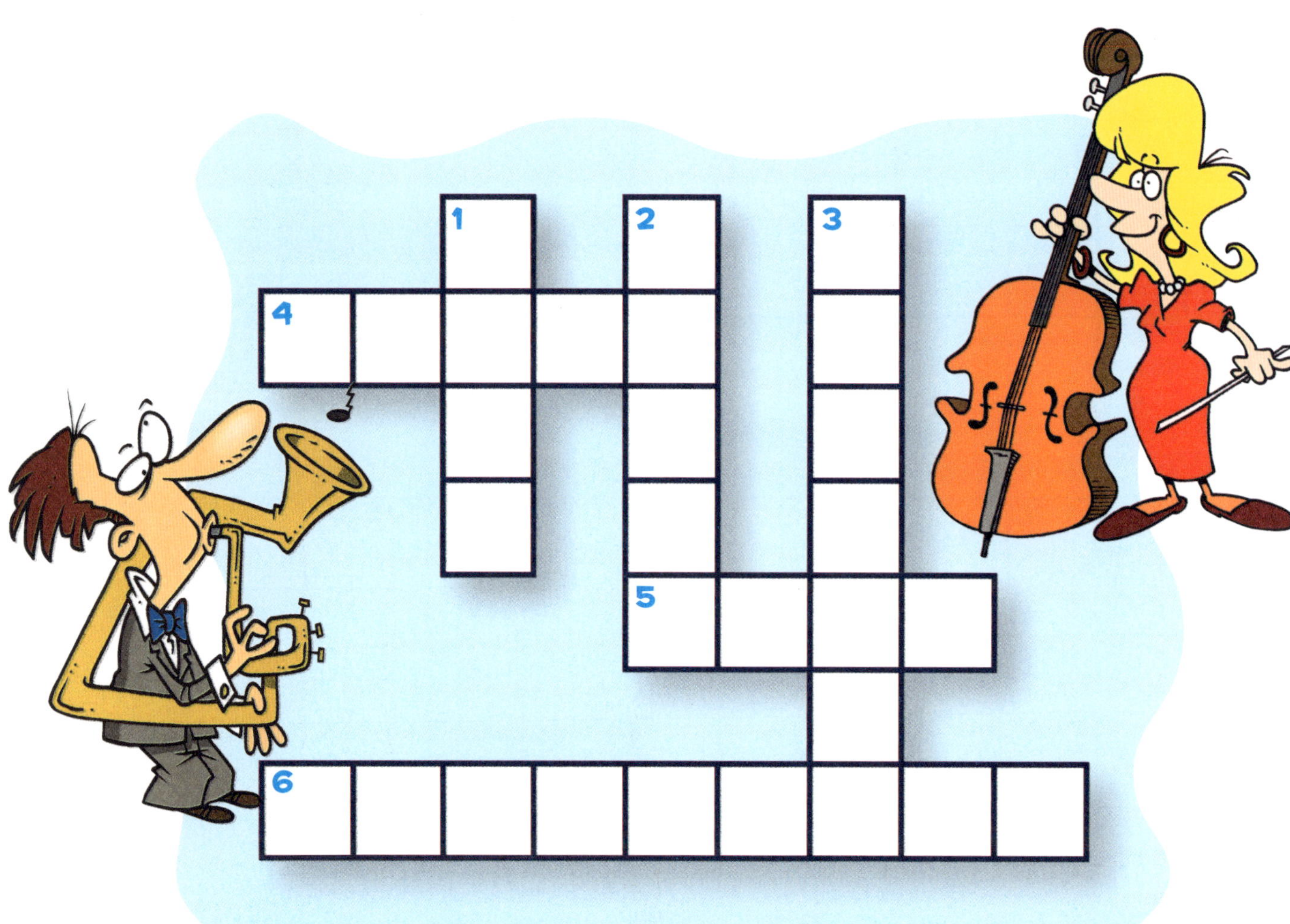

Answers on Page 208

Decode-a-Message

Use the code key below to find something that has to do with grooming.

___ ___ ___ ___   ___ ___ ___ ___ ___,
4 2 8 11   5 6 7 2 13

___ ___ ___ ___
1 6 10 12

___ ___ ___ ___ ___ ___ ___ ___.
5 6 3 6 11 11 6 9

Answers on Page 208

Double Skydivers

Can you find the two pictures that are exactly alike?

Answers on Page 208

Veterinarian

Can you make **25** words or more from the following word?

VETERINARIAN

Answers on Page 208

Even Plane Maze

Fly this plane to the runway by choosing the correct path made of **EVEN** numbers only. You can only go **UP**, **DOWN**, and **ACROSS**—not diagonally.

Start

12	16	2	8	10
6	1	5	11	2
4	22	18	3	13
8	19	6	10	14
7	16	22	9	20
12	5	13	21	12
4	8	16	2	6
10	3	6	11	7

Finish

Answers on Page 209

What Time Is It?

Use the pictures below to complete this crossword puzzle.

Answers on Page 209

Fun For All

Solve this rebus puzzle to find out something that happens when you're having fun.

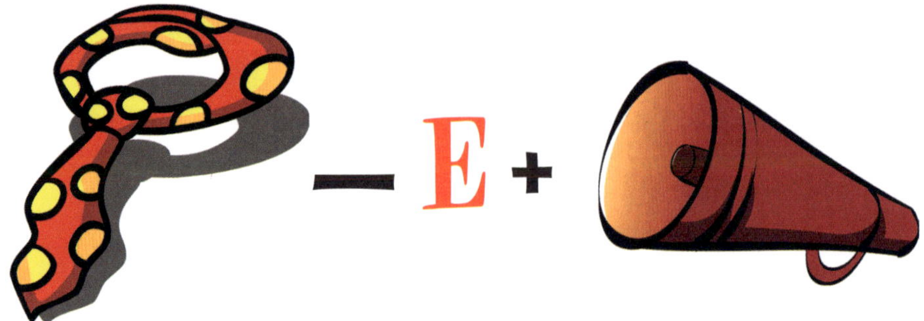

— GA — PHONE

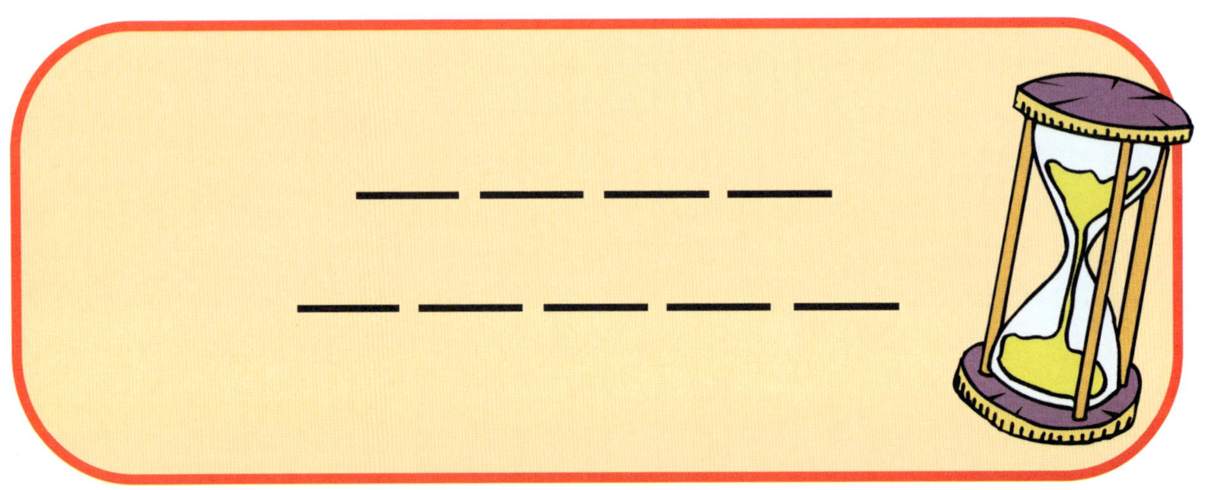

Answers on Page 209

Double Apples

Can you find the two pictures that are exactly alike?

Answers on Page 209

Pretty Peacocks

Find **10** differences between the picture on the left and the one on the right.

Answers on Page 210

Pyramids

Search, find, and circle these **10** things.

ALIENS (2)
BIRDS' NEST
CHEERLEADER
DUCKS (2)
FIRE HYDRANT
MONKEY
MAGNIFYING GLASS
GINGERBREAD MAN
PIE
SNORKEL

Answers on Page 210

Word Scramble

Unscramble each of these words using the clues.

VAERBEEG
(Thirst quencher)

_ _ _ _ _ _ _ _

GIISHATNKGVN
(Holiday)

_ _ _ _ _ _ _ _ _ _ _ _

REOEIHN
(Female hero)

_ _ _ _ _ _ _

OEOTCSINRNVA
(Long chat)

_ _ _ _ _ _ _ _ _ _ _ _

YSYSEDO
(Epic journey)

_ _ _ _ _ _ _

ELADTOR
(Ballerina wear)

_ _ _ _ _ _ _

BHRMAUEGR
(Goes with fries)

_ _ _ _ _ _ _ _ _

OGBIWLN
(Rolling game)

_ _ _ _ _ _ _

Answers on Page 210

Healthy Food

Find these types of healthy food in this word search. Look up, down, backward, forward, and diagonally.

FRUIT	WHOLE GRAIN
VEGETABLES	RAISINS
BEANS	GRANOLA
FIBER	YOGURT
NUTS	CHICKEN

R	A	I	S	I	N	S	K	D	V	E	Z	M
Q	R	E	B	I	F	X	O	R	S	Y	A	X
S	T	O	V	F	D	G	E	T	O	L	L	V
N	J	F	N	E	R	F	Q	G	Q	W	O	E
A	P	Z	I	U	H	U	U	H	H	C	N	G
E	Z	W	A	X	T	R	I	O	K	U	A	E
B	U	B	M	D	T	S	L	T	S	R	R	T
G	D	W	M	Z	W	E	D	J	G	X	G	A
S	S	P	G	Y	G	N	X	S	J	T	M	B
G	F	J	N	R	R	R	X	T	X	N	U	L
G	C	S	A	P	I	Z	B	J	M	V	W	E
Q	Y	I	C	H	I	C	K	E	N	I	D	S
M	N	Y	Q	E	K	W	I	A	C	J	O	E

Answers on Page 211

Fill in the empty squares so that each row, column, and square box contains the numbers **1 - 9** only once.

3	2	1	4		5		6	
6			2		1		5	
	7	5		8	6	2		4
		6	7			5		8
7	5				4			9
1		8	5		9	7		6
		7		3	8	4	9	
8			6		2	3		5
	4		9		7	6	8	1

Answers on Page 211

Building a House

Use the clues below to complete this crossword puzzle.

ACROSS

2 Outdoor room
4 Cover it all
6 Cover the walls and floor
9 Lowest level
10 Keep you warm
11 Hang out
12 Open, close, see through

DOWN

1 Walk right through
3 Separates rooms
5 Cook up a meal
7 Cover the roof
8 Where people sleep

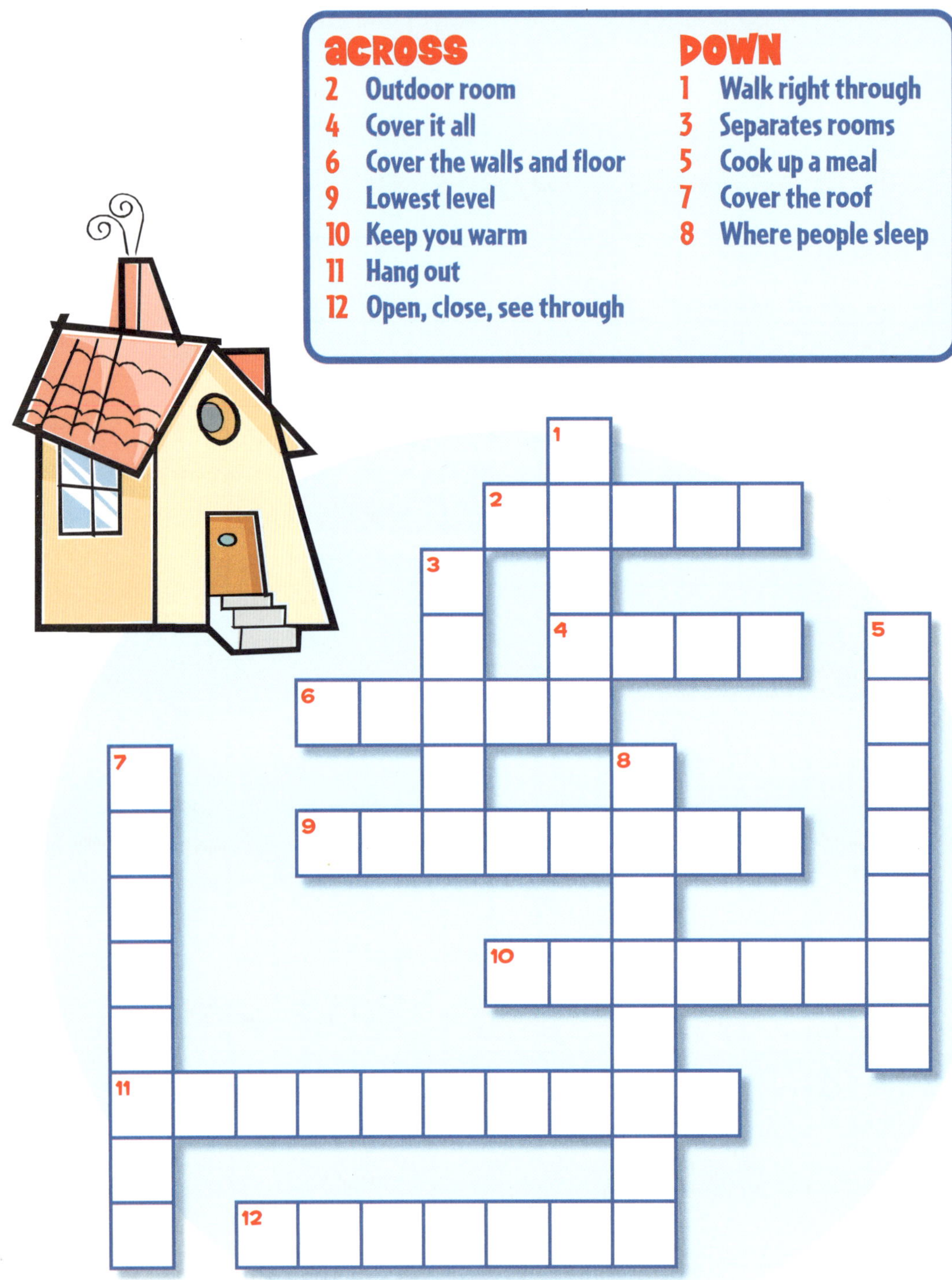

Answers on Page 211

Decode-a-Riddle

Use the key code below to decode and solve this riddle.

A=!	H=*	O=>	V=?
B=@	I=(	P=[	W=/
C=#	J=+	Q=]	X=\
D=$	K=)	R=“	Y=}
E=%	L=;	S=”	Z={
F=^	M=:	T=‘	
G=&	N=<	U=’	

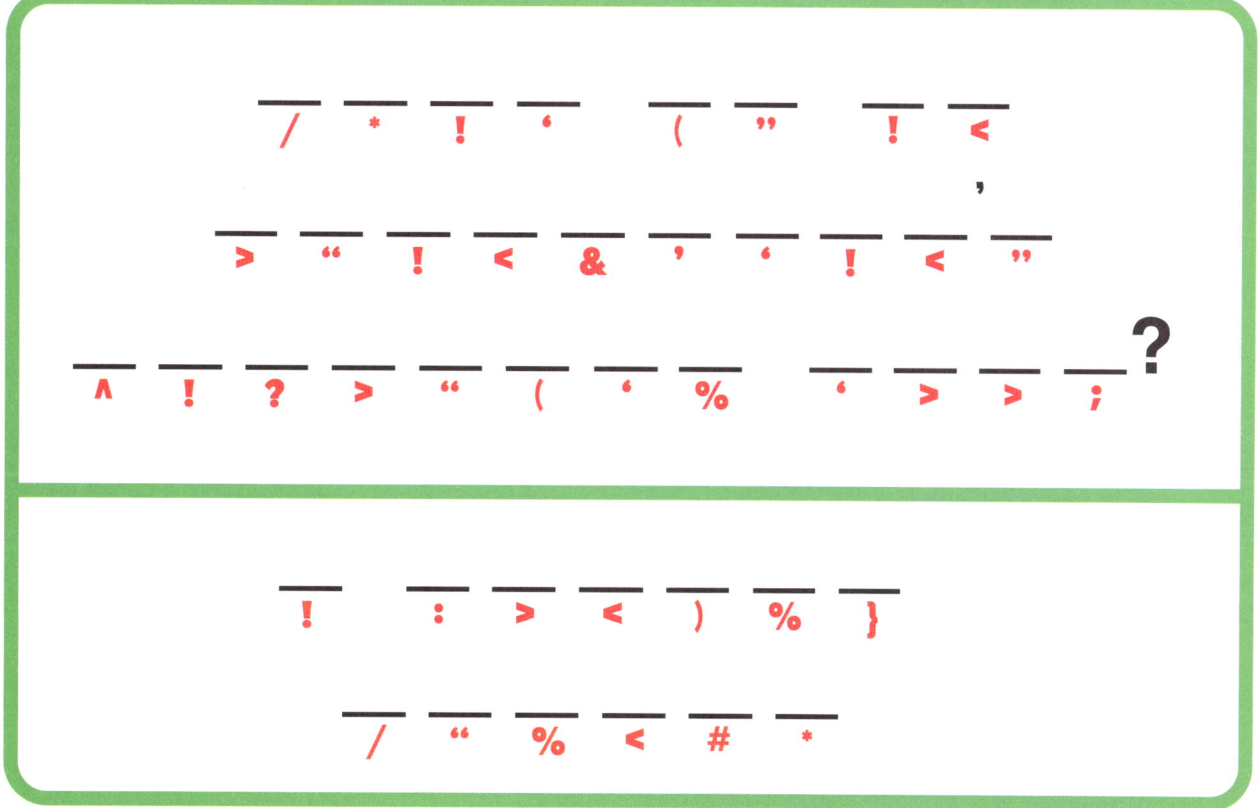

Answers on Page 211

Animal Habitats

Draw a line between the animals in the first column that belong in the habitats in the second column.

Answers on Page 212

Dinnertime

Can you make **25** words or more from the following word?

DINNERTIME

Answers on Page 212

Get to Class on Time

Help this student get to class on time by following the path from **Start** to **Finish**. Watch out for any dead ends along the way—she doesn't want to be late!

Answers on Page 212

In the Cupboard

Use the pictures below to complete this crossword puzzle.

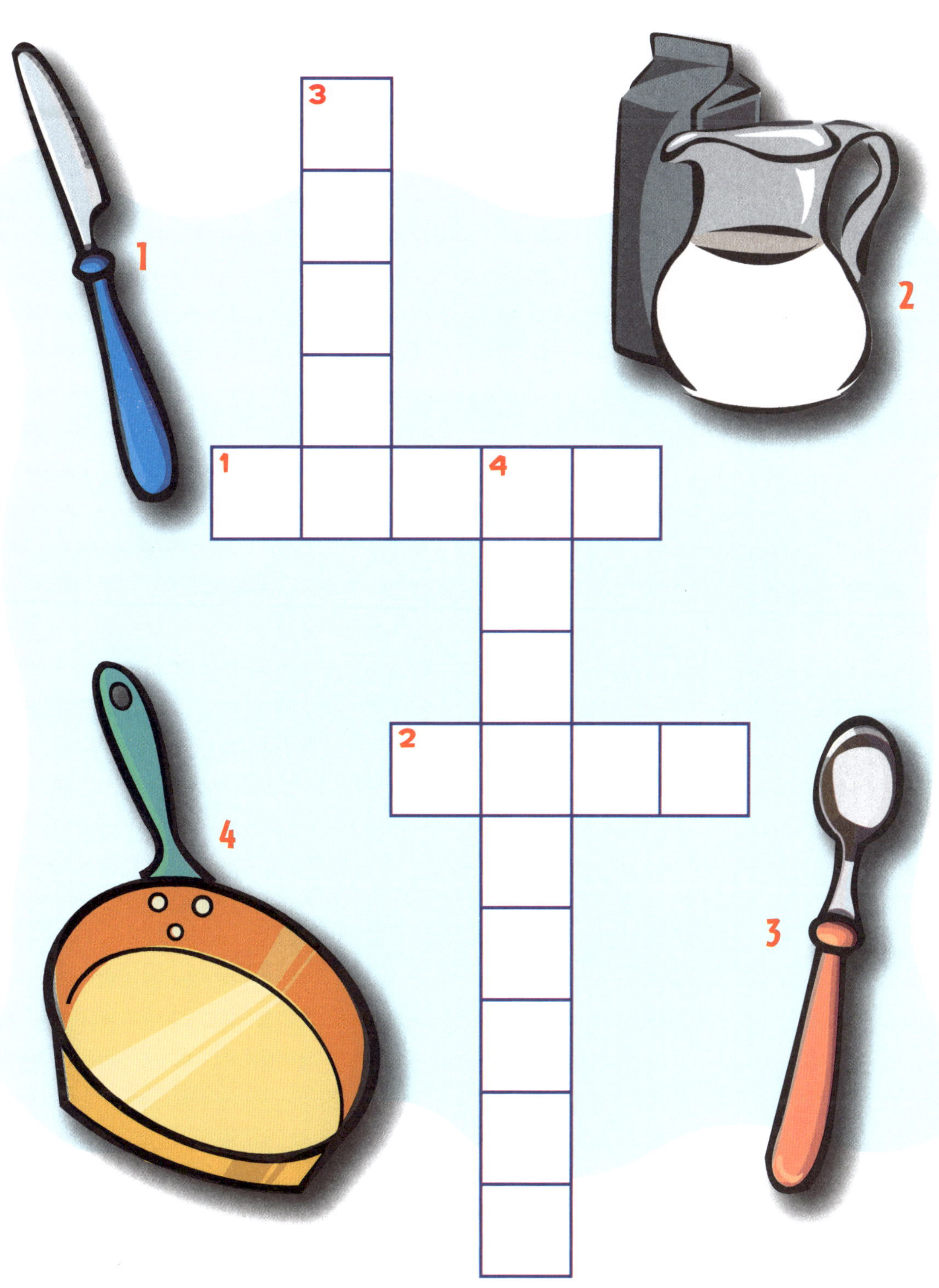

Answers on Page 212

Name of a Leader

Solve this rebus puzzle to find out the name of a leader.

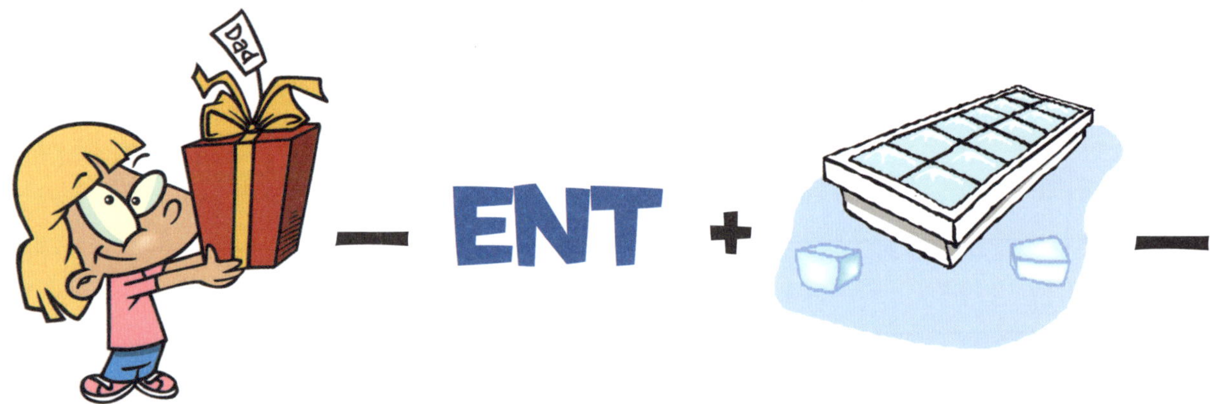

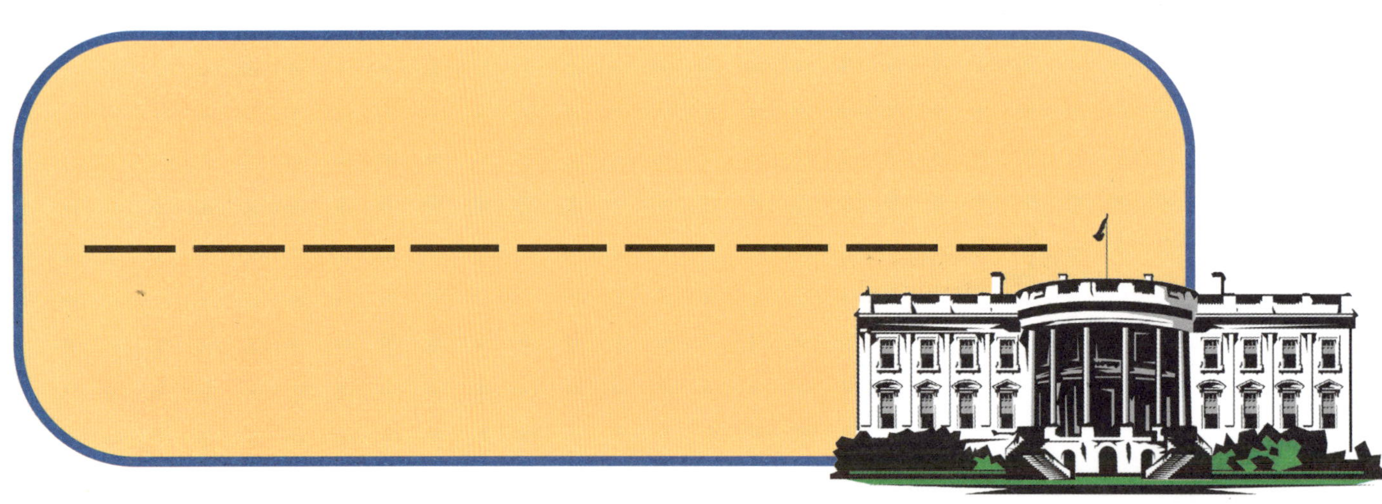

Answers on Page 213

School Bus

Find **two sets of two objects** that rhyme with each other.

Answers on Page 213

Track and Field

Find these things that have to do with track and field in the word search. Look up, down, backward, forward, and diagonally.

Running	Endurance
Hurdle	Relay
Start	Interval
Finish	Spikes
Crossbar	Training

O	R	D	M	I	O	C	J	L	G	K	Y	T	E
T	E	I	H	Z	N	T	K	N	N	L	W	R	J
U	L	U	P	C	B	T	I	X	S	X	K	W	B
S	A	E	D	I	O	N	E	T	Z	M	L	H	E
E	Y	A	U	J	I	B	A	R	X	R	M	V	G
Y	N	T	C	A	D	R	B	P	V	H	G	L	C
R	Z	D	R	L	T	S	J	R	G	A	O	I	L
U	L	T	U	E	L	D	R	U	H	K	L	C	T
N	N	N	D	R	S	P	I	K	E	S	F	J	X
N	L	W	T	N	A	Y	V	X	X	J	L	W	M
I	E	Z	Z	K	S	N	F	Q	Y	B	D	L	V
N	F	I	N	I	S	H	C	H	M	K	J	A	T
G	M	P	A	I	O	P	D	E	R	A	M	I	N
N	L	R	A	B	S	S	O	R	C	U	E	E	S

Answers on Page 213

More State Capitals

Put the capital of each state in the crossword puzzle below.

Answers on Page 213

Lemonade Stand

Search, find, and circle these **10** things.

FROG	FIRE HYDRANT	GINGERBREAD MAN
GOPHERS (2)	MICE (7)	SQUIRREL
PILLOW	OWL	UFO
	PORCUPINE	

Answers on Page 214

Word Scramble

Unscramble each of these words using the clues.

SOGOE
(Bird)

_ _ _ _ _

YDINW
(Air moving)

_ _ _ _ _

TRAGUI
(Instrument)

_ _ _ _ _ _

JNUAC
(Spicy style)

_ _ _ _ _

BITRBA
(Twitchy animal)

_ _ _ _ _ _

EHUSO
(Dwelling)

_ _ _ _ _

Answers on Page 214

Classic Books

Find these name of classic books in this word search. Look up, down, backward, forward, and diagonally.

A	S	Z	Y	H	D	U	X	E	L	O	F	D	V	D
Q	L	F	J	M	K	L	K	Y	Y	X	G	Z	X	N
Z	K	J	P	A	B	K	N	Z	X	K	I	U	L	A
B	O	N	Z	C	X	E	Y	H	D	P	B	T	I	L
U	L	F	B	Q	V	D	G	J	T	F	C	G	T	S
K	D	A	O	I	H	C	C	O	N	I	P	Y	T	I
T	U	P	C	D	J	H	C	Z	M	V	U	B	L	E
T	T	I	L	K	R	N	J	V	O	J	A	W	E	R
B	B	B	I	A	B	A	T	G	Q	X	Q	T	W	U
W	P	W	Q	F	E	E	Z	L	P	J	W	G	O	S
K	H	F	K	W	A	Z	A	I	J	R	K	K	M	A
C	S	R	P	A	X	K	V	U	W	O	Q	S	E	E
C	M	D	B	O	Y	T	M	J	T	E	E	T	N	R
H	X	F	V	O	P	Y	K	T	R	Y	H	W	S	T
F	T	A	Z	F	I	O	W	F	Y	Y	I	T	U	Q

Answers on Page 214

Sudoku

Fill in the empty squares so that each row, column, and square box contains the numbers 1 - 9 only once.

8	4	2	9			6		
	1	9		8	6		3	4
6		3	7		4			2
3			5		2		9	6
	6							
9		5	6		1	3		
1	9		4		5	8		3
4		7	8	3		1	6	
5			1			2	4	9

Answers on Page 214

Time to Laugh

Use the clues below to complete this crossword puzzle.

ACROSS

2 Little laugh

7 ____–____ who's there?

8 Silly questions and answers

DOWN

1 Show your teeth

3 Animated shows

4 In the circus

5 Stand-up guy

6 Tell me funny ones

Answers on Page 215

Decode-a-Message

Use the code key below to find a message that has to do with a cave.

A=6	G=10	N=1	T=4
D=2	H=3	O=7	U=11
E=8	I=5	R=14	
F=13	L=12	S=9	

_ _ _ _ _   _ _   _
4 3 8 14 8   5 9   6

_ _ _ _ _   _ _   _ _ _
12 5 10 3 4   6 4   4 3 8

_ _ _   _ _   _ _ _
8 1 2   7 13   4 3 8

_ _ _ _ _ _.
4 11 1 1 8 12

Answers on Page 215

Double Cats

Can you find the two pictures that are exactly alike?

Answers on Page 215

Alphabet Soup

Can you make **25** words or more from the following phrase?

ALPHABET SOUP

Answers on Page 215

Lucky Number 18

Going from **Start** to **Finish**, choose the path made up of the number **18** only.

18	12	13	17	13
18	12	12	15	15
18	18	12	14	13
17	18	18	17	19
14	15	18	12	17
19	13	18	18	18

Finish

Answers on Page 216

Sudoku

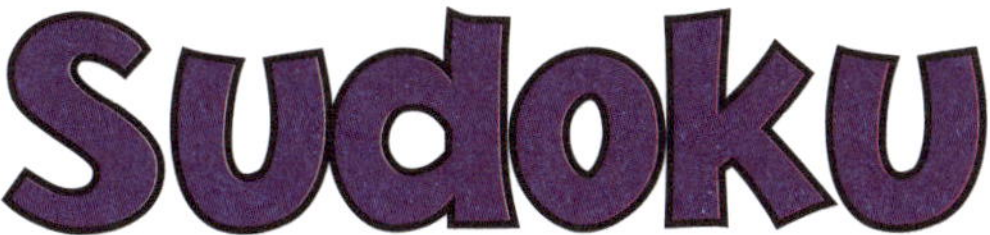

Fill in the empty squares so that each row, column, and square box contains the numbers **1 - 4** only once.

		4	
1			
			4
	3		

Answers on Page 216

Small Pet

Solve this rebus puzzle to find out the name of a small pet.

— PS + —

— EBRA + — M +

— OG

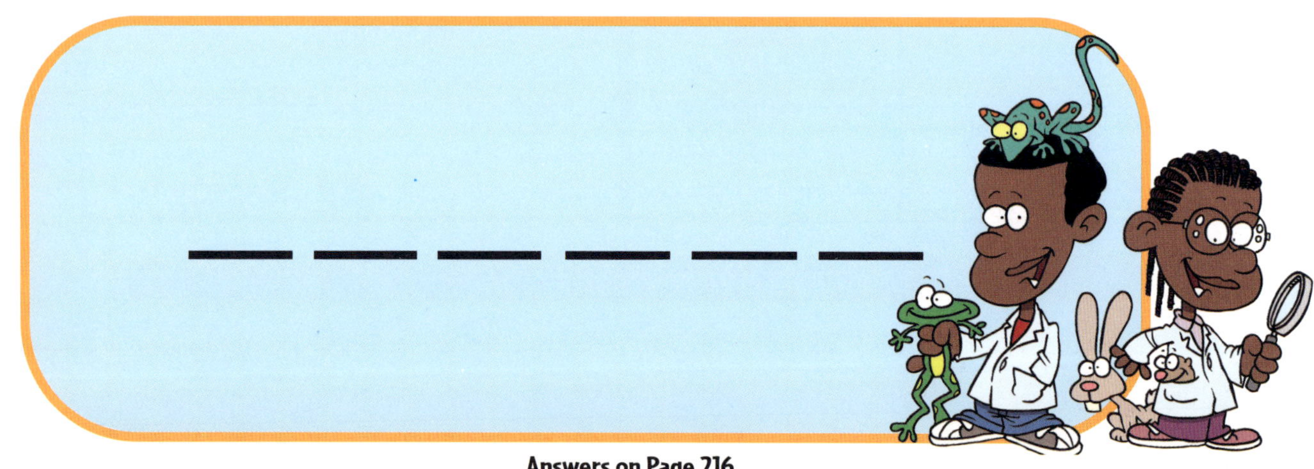

Answers on Page 216

Scientific

Can you make **25** words or more from the following word?

SCIENTIFIC

Answers on Page 216

A Pirate's Life

Find **10** differences between the picture on the left and the one on the right.

Answers on Page 217

Funny Farm

Search, find, and circle these **10** things.

ACORN	DEER	RAKE
BEACH BALL	FLIES (3)	SNAIL
BEES (3)	LIZARDS (2)	SUNGLASSES
	NECKTIE	

Answers on Page 217

Library Number

Guide this man to the library. Just follow the path of numbers that add up to **25**.

Start →

		1	1	1	1	3
		2		2		1
		2		1		2
1	3	1	1	1	2	1
1		1		2		2
1	1	1	1	1	1	2
		3		1		
		1	1	5		

Finish →

Answers on Page 217

Ocean Wildlife

Find these types of ocean wildlife in the word search. Look up, down, backward, forward, and diagonally.

Answers on Page 218

Multiplication

Use the clues below to complete this crossword puzzle.

ACROSS	DOWN
1 6 x 3 =	1 40 x 2 =
2 9 x 1 =	3 4 x 5 =

Answers on Page 218

Read All About It

Use the clues below to complete this crossword puzzle.

ACROSS

3 Pictures and words
6 Out every day
7 Write it for school
9 Rhymes sometimes
10 Performed on a stage

DOWN

1 Weekly or monthly
2 Between two covers
4 Read it on screen
5 Small tale
8 Full-length fiction book

Answers on Page 218

Decode-a-Riddle

Use the code key below to decode and solve this riddle.

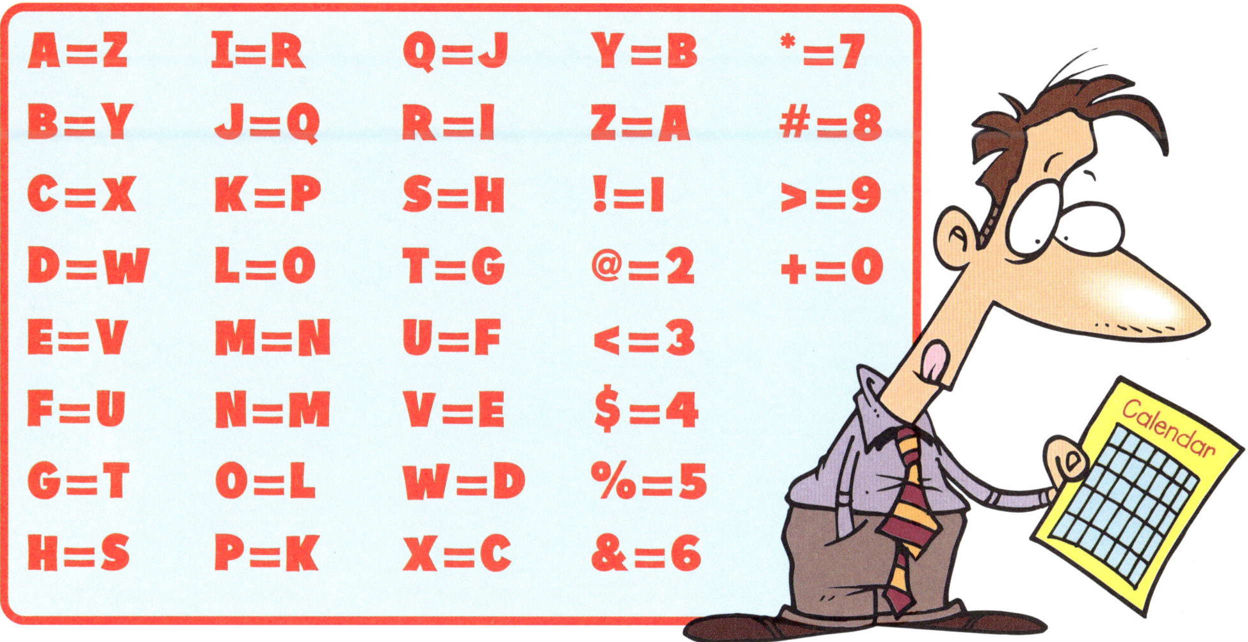

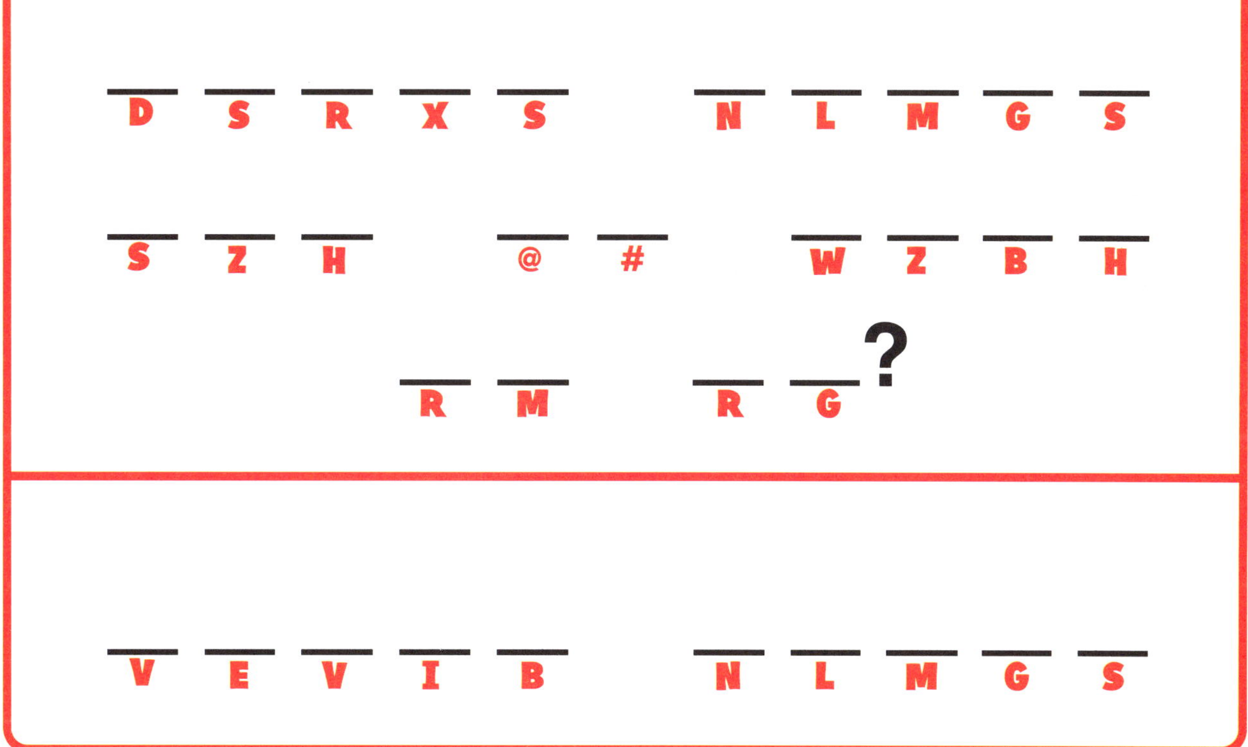

Answers on Page 218

Double Gumballs

Can you find the two pictures that are exactly alike?

Answers on Page 219

Rattlesnake

Can you make **25** words or more from the following word?

RATTLESNAKE

Answers on Page 219

Alien Odd Maze

Guide this alien to the spaceship by choosing the path made of **ODD** numbers only. You can only go **UP**, **DOWN**, and **ACROSS**—not diagonally.

Start

6	21	5	
7	3	8	2
15	10	16	8
1	7	13	1
16	8	9	6
4	6	5	2
11	11	3	1
3	4	5	2

Finish

Answers on Page 219

Post Office

Use the pictures below to complete this crossword puzzle.

Answers on Page 219

Type of Book

Solve this rebus puzzle to discover a type of helpful book.

– AR – ST +

– B – E + – F – I

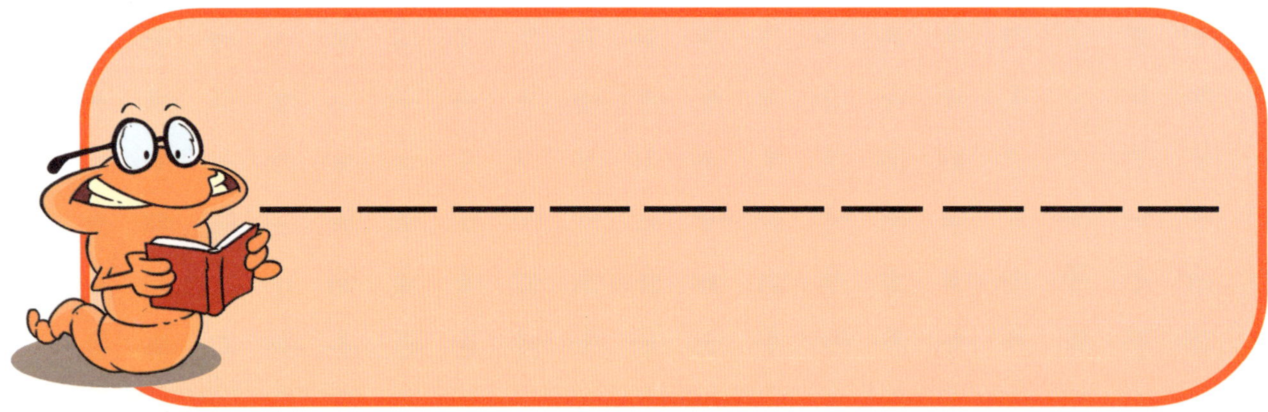

Answers on Page 220

Farm Animals

Find these farm animals in the word search.
Look up, down, backward, forward, and diagonally.

PIG	COW
HORSE	GOAT
SHEEP	DUCK
ROOSTER	GEESE
CHICKEN	DOG

M	F	Z	E	K	Z	U	J	G	M	W	O	B
E	J	M	C	Y	C	H	I	C	K	E	N	Z
O	Q	U	C	N	X	N	R	Q	I	A	V	T
Z	D	S	Y	C	J	U	O	L	F	K	V	K
K	A	Y	S	V	Y	P	O	X	T	K	D	E
G	B	R	T	B	H	U	S	W	R	H	Q	D
J	D	D	B	J	J	W	T	Q	E	Y	R	S
S	Y	O	V	K	O	X	E	G	Z	W	Z	H
H	T	U	G	C	W	N	R	J	F	C	E	O
E	J	G	H	Y	R	S	C	P	R	P	S	R
E	G	O	O	E	O	Y	Q	U	I	L	E	S
P	O	A	C	U	X	Q	V	G	W	L	E	E
K	R	T	U	E	F	E	A	J	W	N	G	Z

Answers on Page 220

Sudoku

Fill in the empty squares so that each row, column, and square box contains the numbers **1-9** only once.

		9		8		6		
	1				6	2		
8					5	7	4	1
		2				8		
1					2		3	
					4			2
	9			6				5
7		5	2				8	
	6		1			4	2	

Answers on Page 220

Double Builders

Can you find the two pictures that are exactly alike?

Answers on Page 220

Hockey Rink

Search, find, and circle these **10** things.

BASEBALLS (5)	DOUGHNUT	LAMPSHADE
CACTUS	EARMUFFS	SNOWMAN
CLARINET	IGLOO	VIDEO CAMERA
	JACK-O'-LANTERN	

Answers on Page 221

Word Scramble

Unscramble each of these words using the clues.

(Create a picture)

_ _ _ _

ETEHT

(They are in your mouth)

_ _ _ _ _

KAFE

(Not real)

_ _ _ _

PALEP

(Round, red fruit)

_ _ _ _ _

ESMRG

(They cause sickness)

_ _ _ _ _

NISGW

(Go back and forth)

_ _ _ _ _

LMKI

(Drink it with cookies)

_ _ _ _

DOCL

(Chilly, freezing)

_ _ _ _

Answers on Page 221

Jungle Animals

Find these jungle animals in this word search. Look up, down, backward, forward, and diagonally.

Answers on Page 221

Fill in the empty squares so that each row, column, and square box contains the numbers **1 - 9** only once.

8	3	1	7			2		
7			2	5				4
		5				6		
3		9			5	7		
	8		3		1	4		2
1	5			7			8	9
5		4		8		9	2	
								6
2	6	8	9	4	3		1	7

Answers on Page 221

Autumn

Use the clues below to complete this crossword puzzle.

ACROSS

1 The air gets ___
4 There is less and less _____
5 The trees get ___
6 Brightly colored leaves
7 Orange vegetables that can be carved
8 Put away light jackets, put on ______
10 Gathering of crops
11 The season to prepare for _____

DOWN

2 What falls in autumn
3 Light up the ____
6 Another name for autumn
9 Can harm delicate plants

Answers on Page 222

Decode-a-Message

What's today's lead story? Use the code key below to find out what happened.

1=A	8=H	15=O	22=V
2=B	9=I	16=P	23=W
3=C	10=J	17=Q	24=X
4=D	11=K	18=R	25=Y
5=E	12=L	19=S	26=Z
6=F	13=M	20=T	
7=G	14=N	21=U	

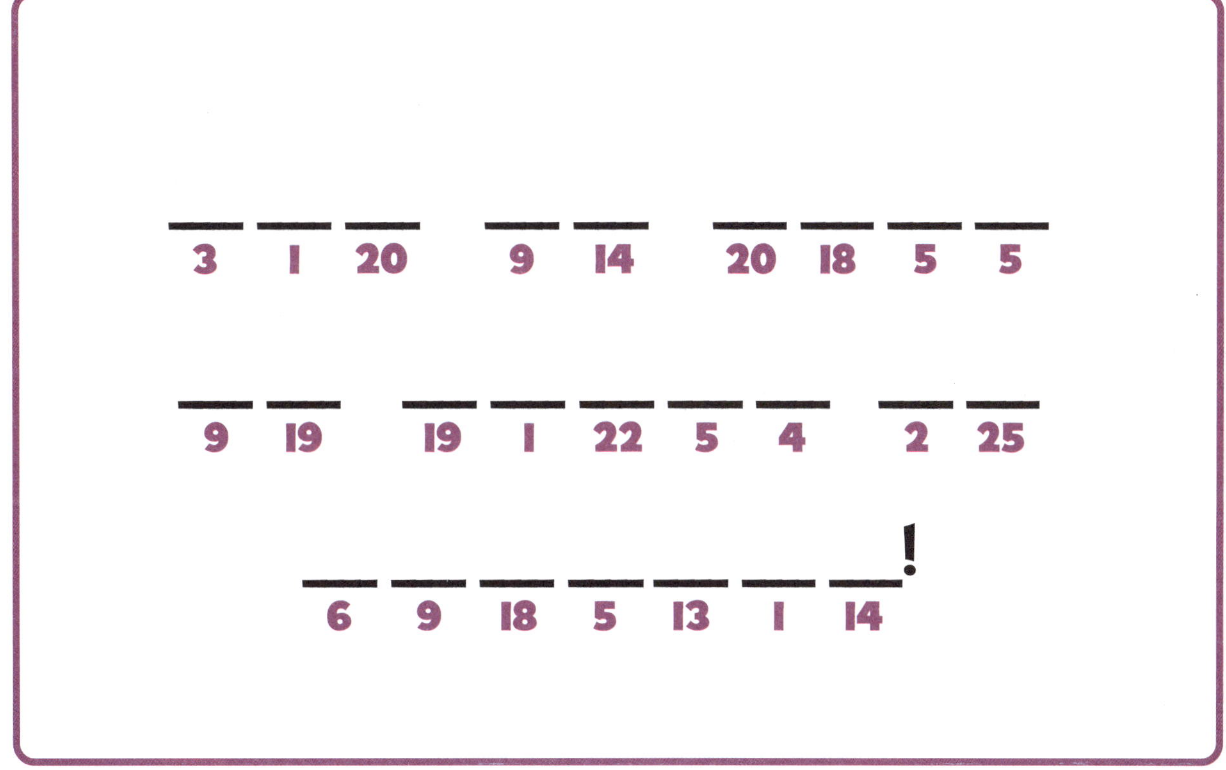

Answers on Page 222

Double Jack-o'-lanterns

Can you find the two pictures that are exactly alike?

Answers on Page 222

Scatterbrain

Can you make **25** words or more from the following word?

Answers on Page 222

Even Maze

Begin at **Start** and make your way to **Finish** by jumping from one **even** number to the next. Move only on even, not odd, numbers. You can only go **UP**, **DOWN**, and **ACROSS**—not diagonally.

Start

2	4	6	7	9	1	3	5
7	9	8	3	5	7	9	1
3	5	6	4	2	3	5	7
9	1	3	5	8	2	4	3
5	7	9	1	3	5	8	9
1	3	5	7	9	1	6	8
7	9	1	3	5	7	9	2
3	5	7	9	1	3	5	4

Answers on Page 223

Types of Vegetables

Find these types of vegetables in this word search.
Look up, down, backward, forward, and diagonally.

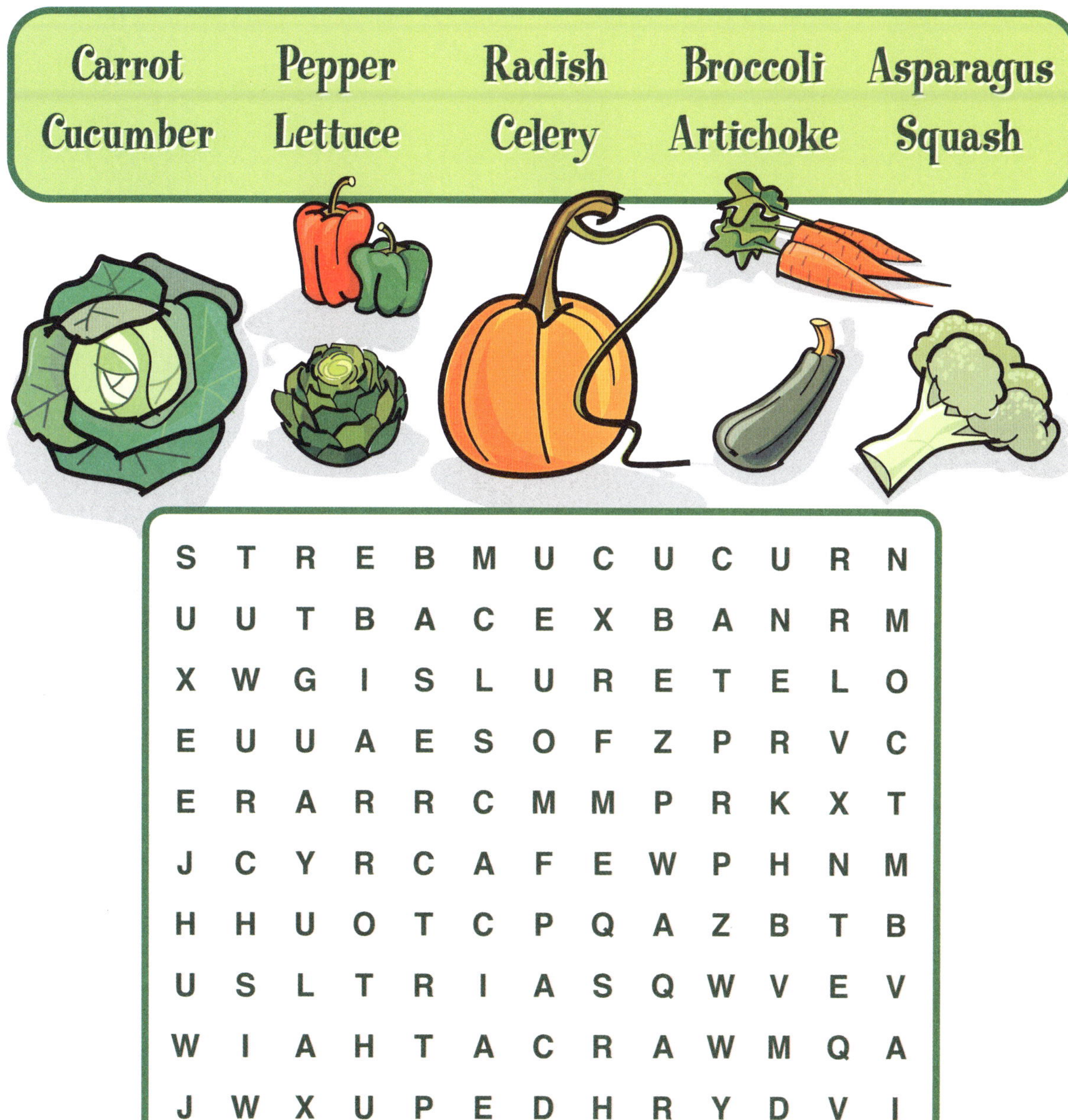

Carrot Pepper Radish Broccoli Asparagus
Cucumber Lettuce Celery Artichoke Squash

S T R E B M U C U C U R N
U U T B A C E X B A N R M
X W G I S L U R E T E L O
E U U A E S O F Z P R V C
E R A R R C M M P R K X T
J C Y R C A F E W P H N M
H H U O T C P Q A Z B T B
U S L T R I A S Q W V E V
W I A H T A C R A W M Q A
J W X U P E D H R Y D V I
V V C R Q E L I O O C V D
F A C U Z S A N S K T N N
K O Q Z M G T Y F H E M V

Answers on Page 223

Family

Solve this rebus puzzle to find a popular expression about the family.

+ IS +

– AL + RE + –

– IMBL + +

– F – H

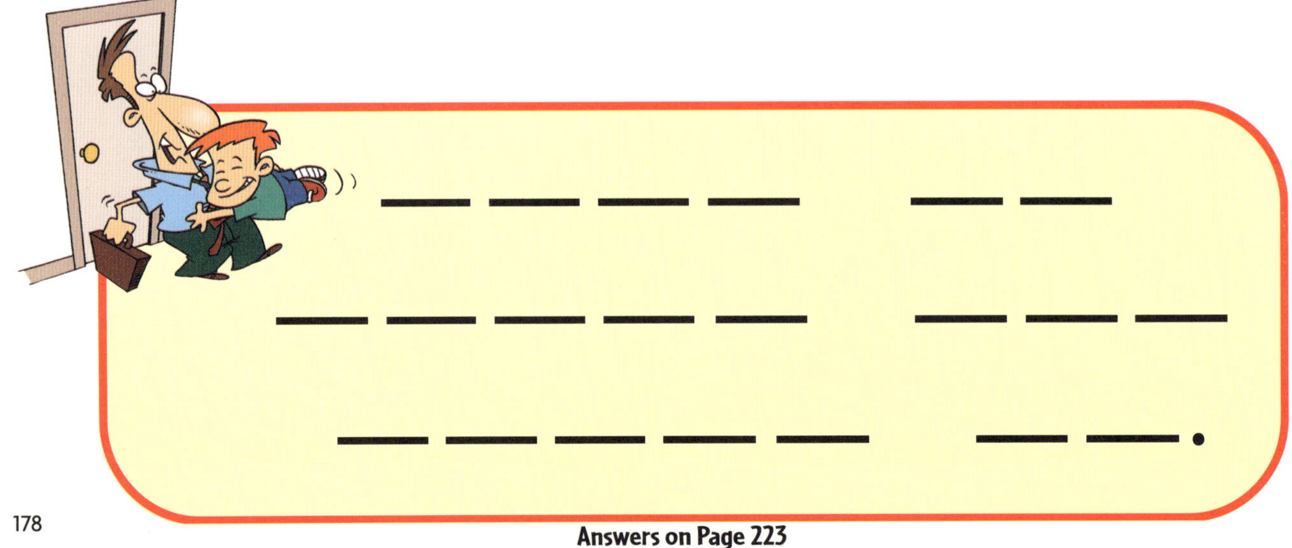

Answers on Page 223

Sudoku

Fill in the empty squares so that each row, column, and square box contains the numbers **1 - 9** only once.

7		3			9			
			7	3	8	5	6	
				6		2		7
		7		4	3			2
	2			7			4	
8				9		7		
1		5		2				
	3	6	4	1	7			
			3			6		1

Answers on Page 223

Answers

Page 4
Rhyme Time

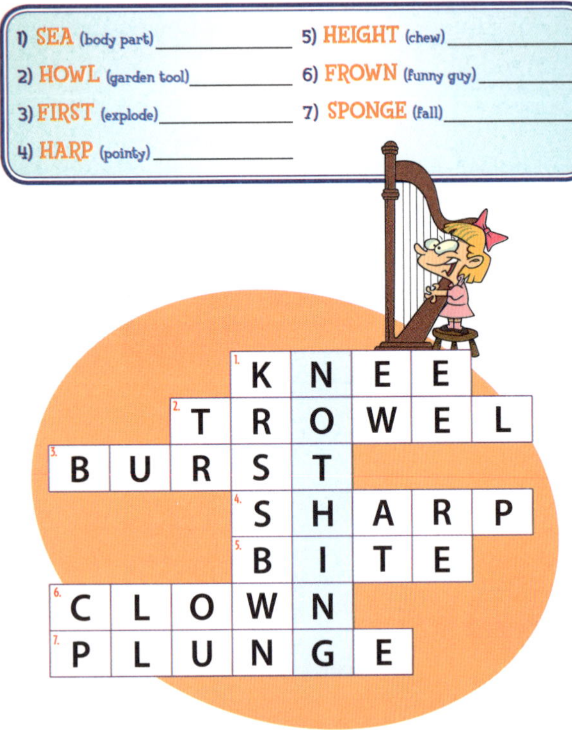

Page 5
In Action

Page 6
Decode-a-Riddle

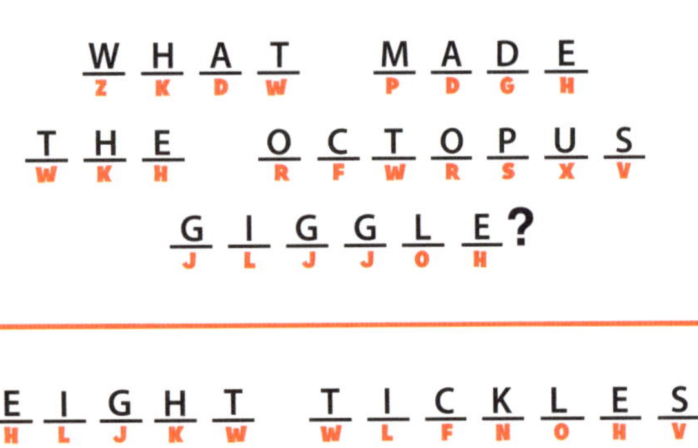

Page 7
Double Popsicles

Answers

Page 8
Fascination

FASCINATION

Here are just a few:

act	coin	fits	sift
acts	cost	icon	sit
ant	cot	inn	sofa
ants	fact	into	soft
can	fan	not	son
cans	fast	oat	taco
cast	fat	oats	tan
cat	fin	sat	tin
cats	fist	scan	ton
coat	fit	scat	tons

Page 9
Musical Mayhem

Page 10
Trucks

Page 11
Poetic Puzzle

Answers

Page 12

Lazy Sunday

Page 13

State Capitals

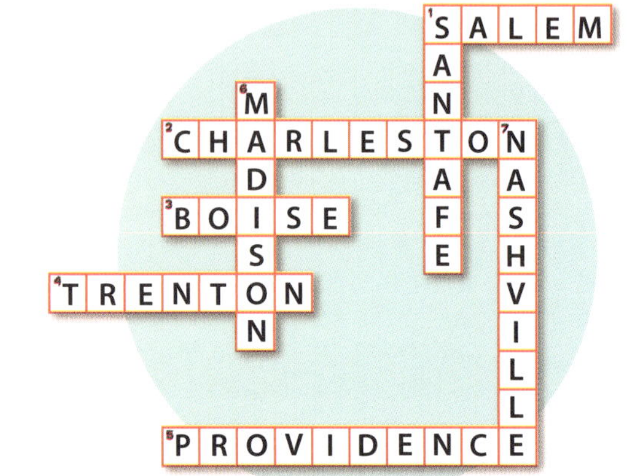

Page 14

Bust-a-Beat

Page 15

Answers

Page 16
Word Scramble

RBID
(Likes to fly)
B I R D

NUJE
(Summer month)
J U N E

CEID
(Number game)
D I C E

TCHAW
(Tells time)
W A T C H

Page 17
Fishing

Page 18
Where Am I?

ACROSS	DOWN
3 Circling	1 Not indoors
5 Hidden in back of	2 Enter the building
6 In the middle	4 Above
7 Beneath	6 Next to

Page 19
Decode-a-Message

A=3	D=9	N=10	R=2
B=11	E=1	O=8	Y=4
C=6	L=5	P=7	

R E D C R A Y O N
2 1 9 6 2 3 4 8 10

Answers

Page 20
Word Game

P O P G O E S
T H E W E A S E L.

Page 21
Celebration

CELEBRATION

Here are just a few:

able	boil	neat	riot
ace	canoe	oat	tea
acne	clone	ocean	teal
acorn	clot	rain	tear
actor	ice	ran	teen
air	icon	rate	ten
alert	into	ratio	tire
aloe	lace	real	tone
bake	learn	reel	tree
baton	nail	rib	
bear	near	rice	

Page 22
Sudoku

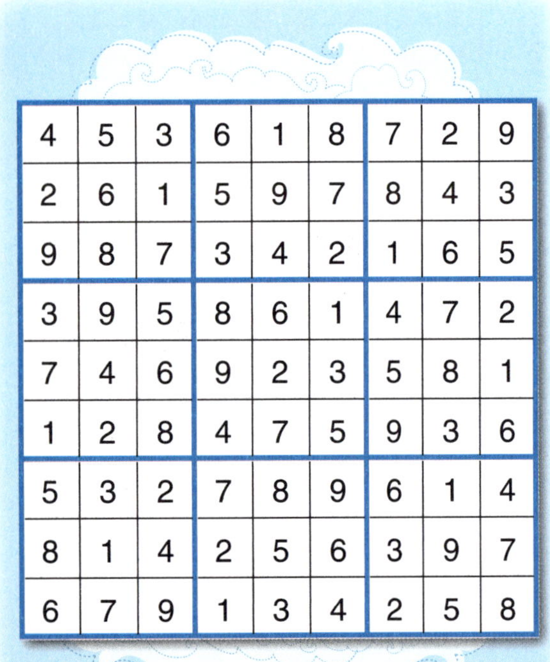

4	5	3	6	1	8	7	2	9
2	6	1	5	9	7	8	4	3
9	8	7	3	4	2	1	6	5
3	9	5	8	6	1	4	7	2
7	4	6	9	2	3	5	8	1
1	2	8	4	7	5	9	3	6
5	3	2	7	8	9	6	1	4
8	1	4	2	5	6	3	9	7
6	7	9	1	3	4	2	5	8

Page 23
Ballerina

Answers

Page 24
Slippery Stuff

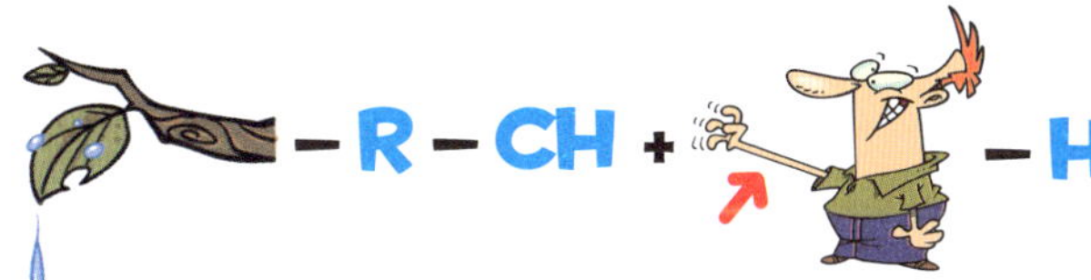

Page 25
Creative Puzzle

B E E ' S
K N E E S.

Page 26
Take a Trip

across
1 You need these for the plane or train
5 Things to remember your trip by
6 Where to eat on a trip
8 Reference for info
9 Pack this up with clothes
10 Book in advance

down
2 Snap those pictures
3 Mail these to your friends
4 Best seats on the plane
7 Leads you in a new place

Page 27
Sudoku

3	9	1	5	8	4	2	7	6
2	5	7	1	3	6	8	4	9
8	6	4	2	9	7	3	5	1
6	8	3	7	2	1	5	9	4
5	7	9	4	6	3	1	2	8
1	4	2	8	5	9	6	3	7
7	3	8	9	1	5	4	6	2
4	2	6	3	7	8	9	1	5
9	1	5	6	4	2	7	8	3

Answers

Page 28
Strike Out

Page 29
Word Scramble

ILDAGFRUE
(Water rescue)
L I F E G U A R D

IMEETTSLO
(Christmas leaves hung in doorway)
M I S T L E T O E

SGNATYM
(Athlete)
G Y M N A S T

NUUAMT
(Season)
A U T U M N

AUMERSETPKR
(Food source)
S U P E R M A R K E T

EAMDMRI
(Fishy person)
M E R M A I D

AAGORKON
(Animal)
K A N G A R O O

ALANSAG
(Food)
L A S A G N A

Page 30
Tennis

Page 31
Lucky NumberThree

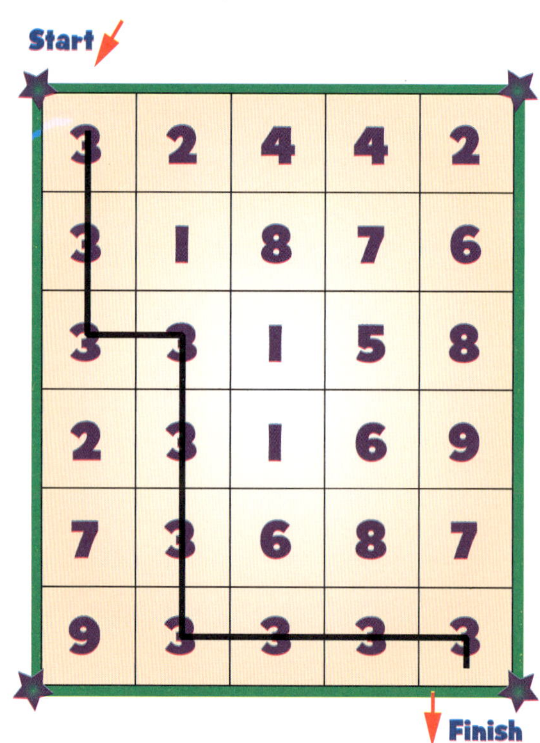

Answers

Page 32

Rescue Vehicles

ACROSS	DOWN
1 Broken leg	4 Burglar
2 House fire	5 Sea distress
3 Search and rescue	

Page 33

Decode-a-Riddle

A=5	E=6	I=2	M=3	S=4
C=11	G=13	K=7	N=12	U=14
D=1	H=9	L=8	P=10	

C	H	I	C	K	E	N		A	N	D
11	9	2	11	7	6	12		5	12	1

D	U	M	P	L	I	N	G	S
1	14	3	10	8	2	12	13	4

Page 34

Double Octopuses

Page 35

A Balanced Diet

A BALANCED DIET

Here are just a few:

acid	dad	idea	nail
aid	dance	lace	need
bad	data	land	net
bald	dead	late	nice
band	dealt	lead	tab
bleed	debit	lean	table
can	deli	lend	tail
canal	dine	lent	tale
candle	eat	lice	tan
cane	elite	lid	tea
dab	ice	lie	tile

Answers

Page 36
Odd Birthday Maze

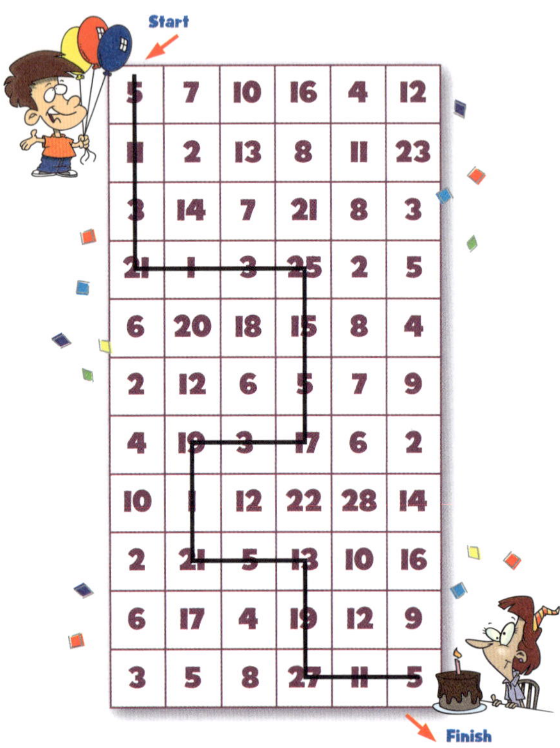

Page 37
Holiday Time

Page 38
Super Singer

Page 39
Hardware Store

Answers

Page 40

Pumpkin Harvest

Page 41

Page 42

U.S. Cities

Page 43

Word Scramble

REFLWO
(Blooming plant)
F L O W E R

HTEGI
(Not seven or nine)
E I G H T

LDSALA
(Texas city)
D A L L A S

LETBLA
(Type of dance)
B A L L E T

GLUJEN
(Land of thick vegetation)
J U N G L E

TROAC
(Pretending professional)
A C T O R

Answers

Page 44

Tools

Page 45

Running Errands

IMOMMOMNMOMEMOMEMOM
DMOMMOMTOMOMGOMOM
MOMTOMOMTMOMHMOMMOM
EMOMPMOMOMOMTMOMTMOMY!

I

N E E D

T O

G O

T O

T H E

P O T T Y!

Page 46

Summer Fun

Page 47

Decode-a-Riddle

1=A	8=H	15=O	22=V
2=B	9=I	16=P	23=W
3=C	10=J	17=Q	24=X
4=D	11=K	18=R	25=Y
5=E	12=L	19=S	26=Z
6=F	13=M	20=T	
7=G	14=N	21=U	

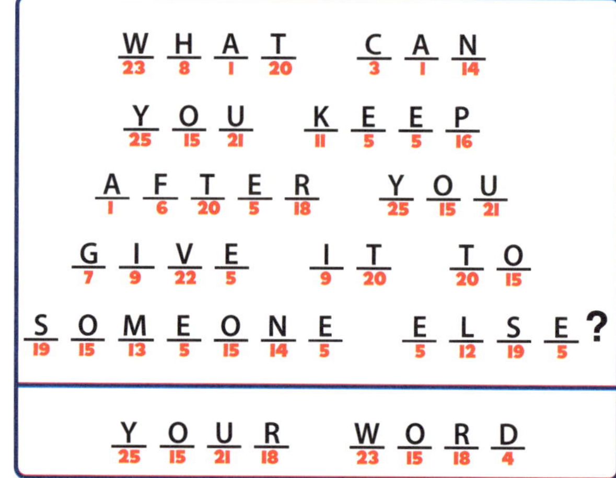

W H A T C A N
23 8 1 20 3 1 14

Y O U K E E P
25 15 21 11 5 5 16

A F T E R Y O U
1 6 20 5 18 25 15 21

G I V E I T T O
7 9 22 5 9 20 20 15

S O M E O N E E L S E?
19 15 13 5 15 14 5 5 12 19 5

Y O U R W O R D
25 15 21 18 23 15 18 4

Answers

Page 48

Double Bananas

Page 49

Agriculture

AGRICULTURE

Here are just a few:

ace	culture	lace	rice
acre	cure	large	rule
age	ear	late	tag
agile	eat	leg	tail
alert	gate	liter	tale
argue	girl	race	tea
cage	glare	rag	teal
car	grail	rage	tear
cat	great	rail	tie
clear	guitar	rate	tiger
cruel	ice	real	urge

Page 50

Shark Maze

Page 51

Animals

Answers

Page 52

Camera Parts

Page 53

Team Time

ACROSS

3 Oakland baseball team
6 Atlanta hockey team
8 Cleveland basketball team
9 St. Louis baseball team
10 LA baseball team

DOWN

1 New York football team
2 Toronto hockey team
4 Dallas football team
5 Boston basketball team
7 New England football team

Page 54

Wonderful Wizards

Page 55

Sudoku

4	2	9	3	7	1	8	5	6
6	5	8	4	2	9	7	1	3
1	7	3	5	6	8	2	9	4
2	8	6	9	5	7	3	4	1
7	9	1	2	4	3	5	6	8
5	3	4	1	8	6	9	7	2
3	6	2	7	9	4	1	8	5
8	1	7	6	3	5	4	2	9
9	4	5	8	1	2	6	3	7

Answers

Page 56
Sticky Stuff

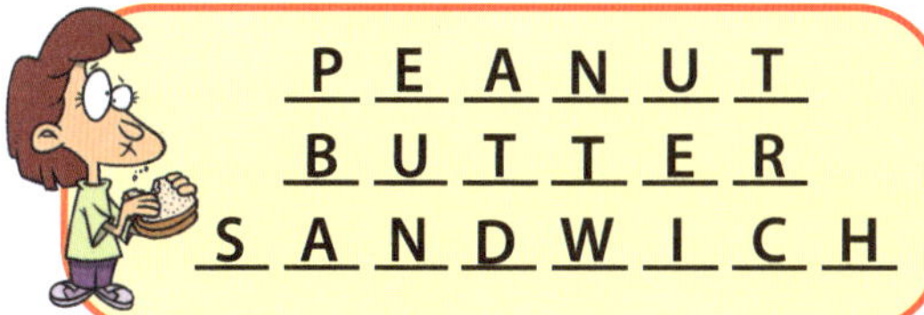

Page 57
Word Scramble

TRENASTUAR
(Eating place)
R E S T A U R A N T

CTYDNRIIAO
(Word describer)
D I C T I O N A R Y

RHCYISMTE
(Class subject)
C H E M I S T R Y

RELIOPCHET
(Aircraft)
H E L I C O P T E R

RPNEAAIL
(Sky coach)
A I R P L A N E

LABLSBAE
(Throwing game)
B A S E B A L L

SMULCE
(Under your skin)
M U S C L E

OOIUYSLLQ
(Singly speaking)
S O L I L O Q U Y

Page 58
Types of Dance

Page 59
Word Game

GIGINGIG

I N B E T W E E N
G I G S

Answers

Page 60

Yummy!

ACROSS

4 Fresh and natural
6 Eat it at your birthday party
7 Frozen sweet treat
9 Thick and chocolaty
10 Liquid ice-cream drink

DOWN

1 Baked chocolate squares
2 Apple, pumpkin, chocolate cream
3 Lots in a box
5 Soft and sweet, chocolate or butterscotch
8 Drink it with cookies

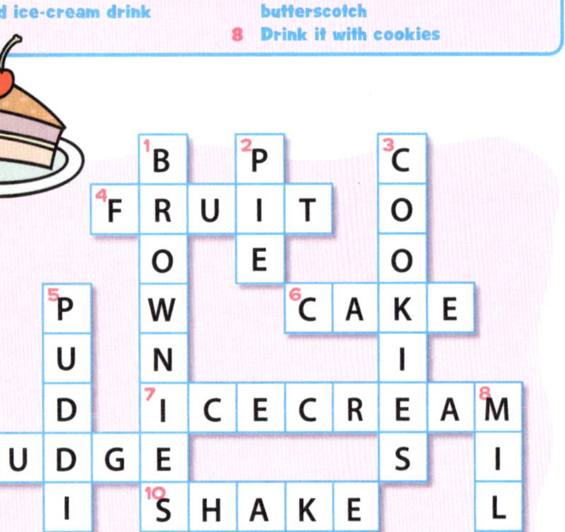

Page 61

Decode-a-Riddle

A=2	H=16	O=13	T=3
C=12	I=7	P=5	U=8
D=4	M=15	R=6	W=14
E=10	N=9	S=11	Y=1

W H E N (14 16 10 9) Y O U (1 13 8) W I S H (14 7 11 16)
U P O N (8 5 13 9) A (2) S T A R, (11 3 2 6)
Y O U R (1 13 8 6) D R E A M S (4 6 10 2 15 11)
C O M E (12 13 15 10) T R U E. (3 6 8 10)

Page 62

Double Ladybugs

Page 63

Engagement

ENGAGEMENT

Here are just a few:

age	man	name
ant	mane	neat
ate	mat	net
eat	mate	tag
egg	me	tame
gag	mean	tan
gage	meat	tea
game	meet	team
gate	mega	tee
gem	men	teen
gene	met	teenage
gnat	nag	ten

Answers

Page 64
Even Bear Maze

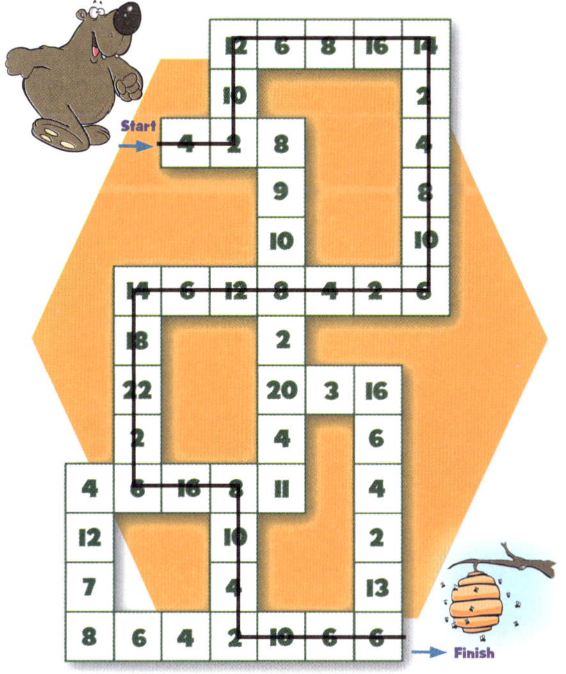

Page 65
Vehicle Sounds

Page 66
Mythical Animal

Page 67
Double Dinosaurs

Answers

Page 68

Safari Trip

Page 69

Page 70

Airplanes

Page 71

Word Scramble

TNCFORON
(Face up against)
C O N F R O N T

LEGRAYL
(Place where art is shown)
G A L L E R Y

TANGINMAIOI
(Creative thinking)
I M A G I N A T I O N

CATINTRATO
(Appeal, pull)
A T T R A C T I O N

CIVDEENE
(Proof)
E V I D E N C E

DUNHATE
(Filled with ghosts)
H A U N T E D

GAGUNALE
(Word of a country)
L A N G U A G E

JASMAAP
(What you wear to bed)
P A J A M A S

Answers

Page 72
Fish

Page 73
Sudoku

8	9	5	7	3	6	2	4	1
1	7	2	5	9	4	3	6	8
4	6	3	1	2	8	9	5	7
2	5	1	4	6	3	8	7	9
9	3	4	8	5	7	1	2	6
7	8	6	2	1	9	5	3	4
6	1	8	3	7	5	4	9	2
5	4	7	9	8	2	6	1	3
3	2	9	6	4	1	7	8	5

Page 74
Thirsty

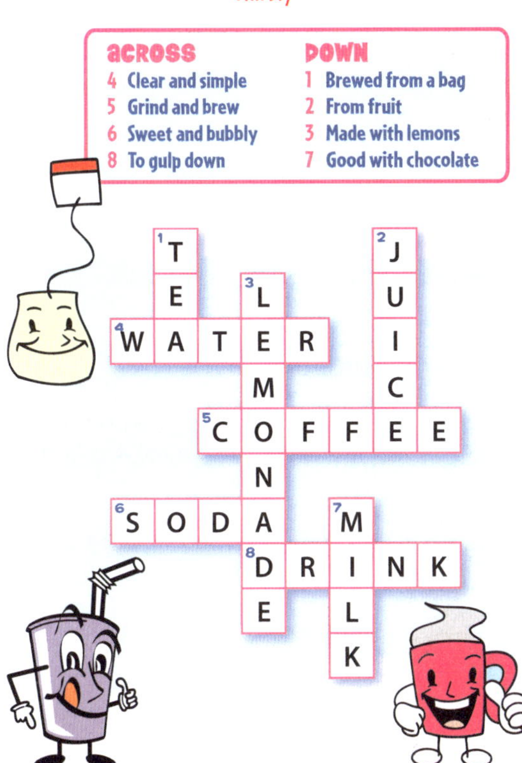

Page 75
Decode-a-Message

A=4 H=3 T=2
C=1 O=5

H O T
3 5 2

C O C O A
1 5 1 5 4

Answers

Page 76

Space Adventures

Page 77

Burglarize

BURGLARIZE

Here are just a few:

air	gab	large	real
argue	gear	leg	rear
bag	gel	liar	regal
bar	girl	lie	rib
barrel	glare	lug	rub
bear	grail	luge	rug
bizarre	grub	lure	rural
blare	gruel	rage	urge
blaze	ire	rail	zag
ear	lab	rale	zeal
err	lag	rare	zig

Page 78

Lucky Number Two

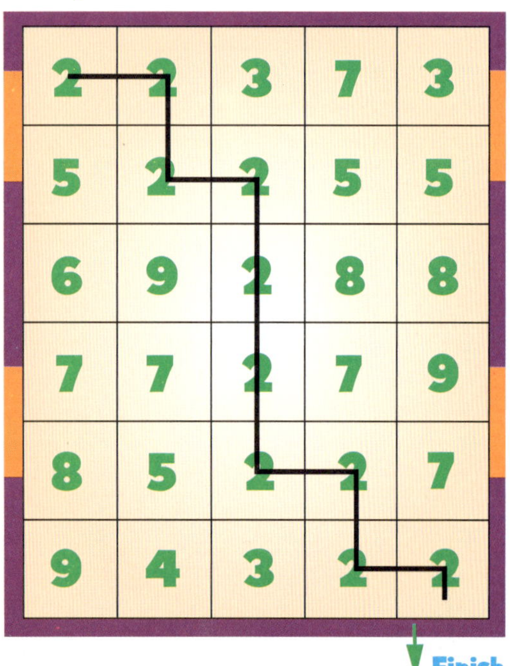

Page 79

State Capitals

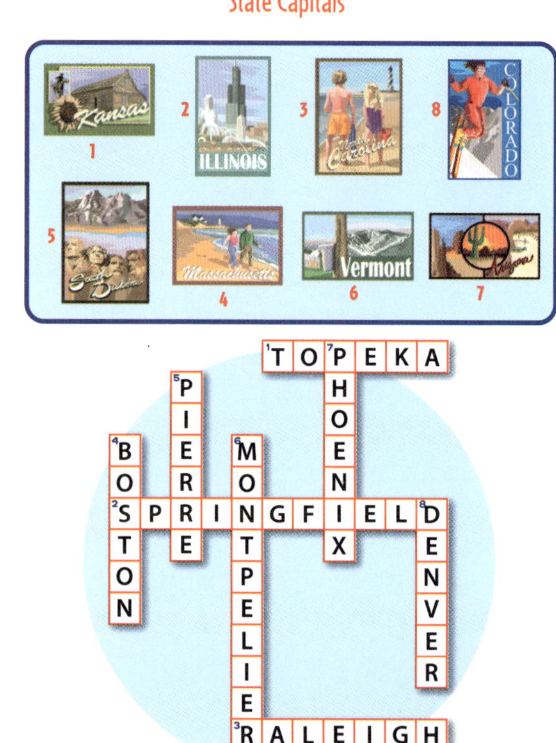

Answers

Page 80
Wet Adventure

Page 81
Opposites Attract

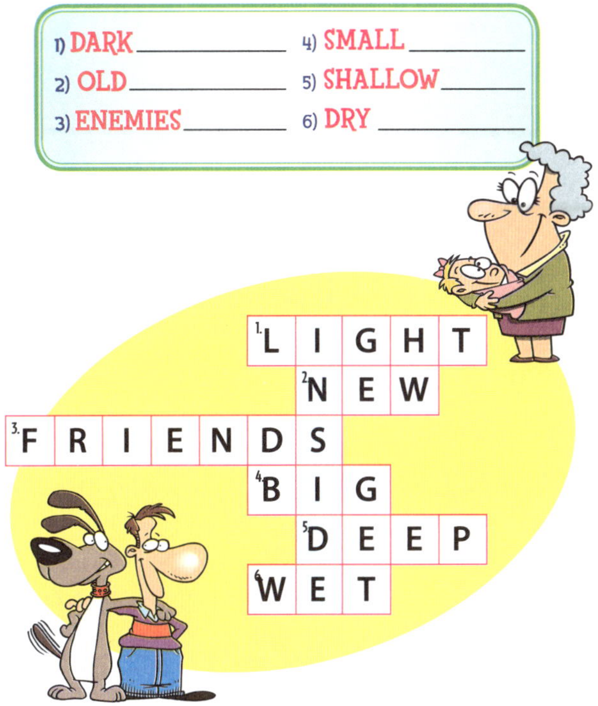

Page 82
Bull's Eye

Page 83
Sudoku

6	5	9	4	1	8	2	3	7
8	7	3	2	6	5	1	9	4
1	4	2	9	7	3	6	5	8
5	8	4	7	2	9	3	6	1
2	9	6	3	4	1	7	8	5
3	1	7	5	8	6	9	4	2
7	2	5	6	3	4	8	1	9
9	6	1	8	5	2	4	7	3
4	3	8	1	9	7	5	2	6

Answers

Page 84
Carnival Fun

Page 85
Word Scramble

TEGILINNS
(Paying attention to)
L I S T E N I N G

YERVNOEE
(All the people)
E V E R Y O N E

RATHEFES
(On a bird)
F E A T H E R S

GIPVIRLEE
(Advantage, special treatment)
P R I V I L E G E

GALMENGI
(Shining)
G L E A M I N G

SELNERLETS
(Persistant, not stopping)
R E L E N T L E S S

PIWRESH
(Speak softly)
W H I S P E R

KRADYABC
(Behind the house)
B A C K Y A R D

Page 86
Bicycle Ride

Page 87
Let's Build

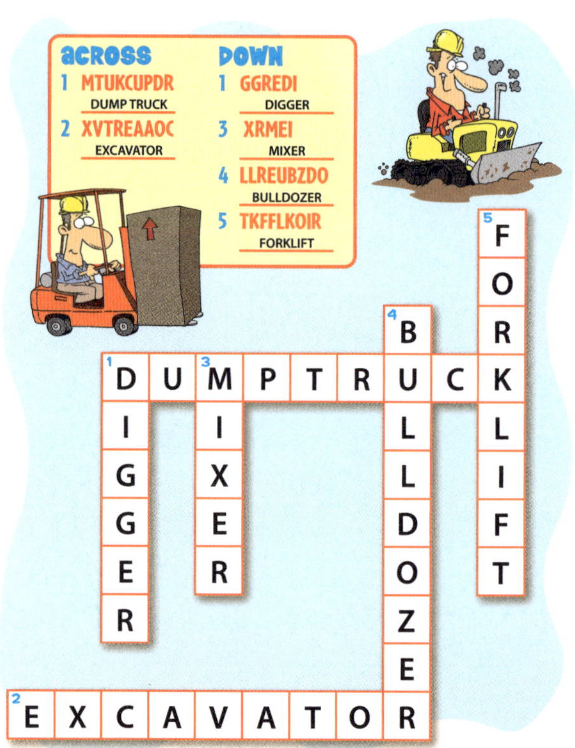

Answers

Page 88

Game Time

ACROSS	DOWN
1 Kings and queens	2 Find the missing item.
5 Toss a ball back and forth.	3 Ready or not, here I come.
8 Hand off the baton	4 Spin the rope, jump
9 Card game with bids	5 Jump my piece.
10 Three water birds	6 You're it!
11 Two hands, no tackling	7 Small glass balls

Page 89

Lunchtime

A=8	F=16	K=9	R=10
B=14	G=1	M=15	S=6
C=11	H=5	N=7	T=12
E=4	I=2	O=3	W=13

GONE FISHING, BACK TOMORROW.

G 1 O 3 N 7 E 4   F 16 I 2 S 6 H 5 I 2 N 7 G 1,

B 14 A 8 C 11 K 9   T 12 O 3 M 15 O 3 R 10 R 10 O 3 W 13.

Page 90

Double Kites

Page 91

Anatomical

ANATOMICAL

Here are just a few:

act	clot	loan	not
action	coal	loin	oat
ail	coat	lot	oil
aim	coil	mail	oilcan
ant	icon	main	on
atom	into	malt	tan
calm	ion	man	tic
can	lima	mania	ton
canal	limo	mic	tonic
clam	lint	mint	
clan	lit	molt	

Answers

Page 92
Odd House Maze

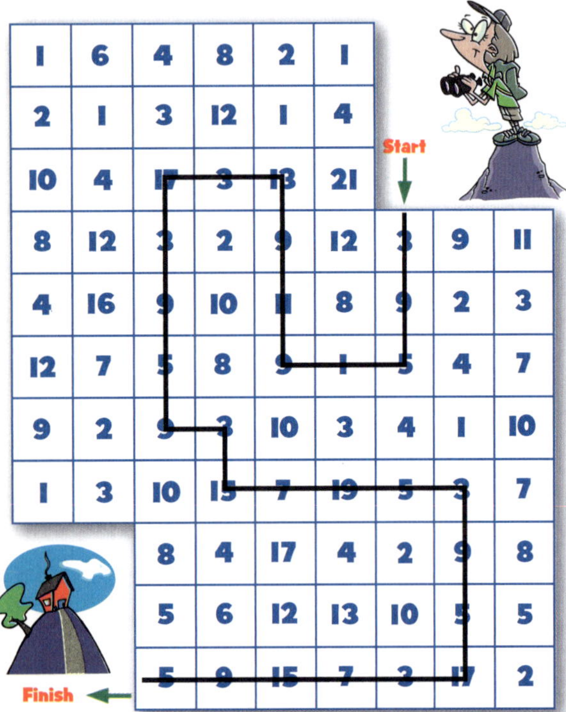

Page 93
Under the Sea

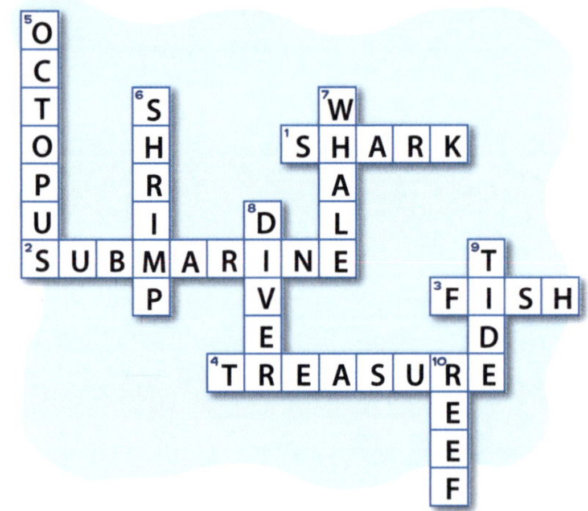

Page 94
On the Go

Page 95
Sudoku

2	3	9	5	8	1	7	4	6
6	4	7	9	2	3	1	5	8
8	1	5	6	4	7	9	3	2
7	5	3	2	1	6	4	8	9
9	8	2	7	5	4	6	1	3
4	6	1	8	3	9	5	2	7
1	9	8	4	7	2	3	6	5
3	2	6	1	9	5	8	7	4
5	7	4	3	6	8	2	9	1

Answers

Page 96
Ice Hockey Game

Page 97

Page 98
Traveling Circus

Page 99
Word Scramble

Answers

Page 100

Car Parts

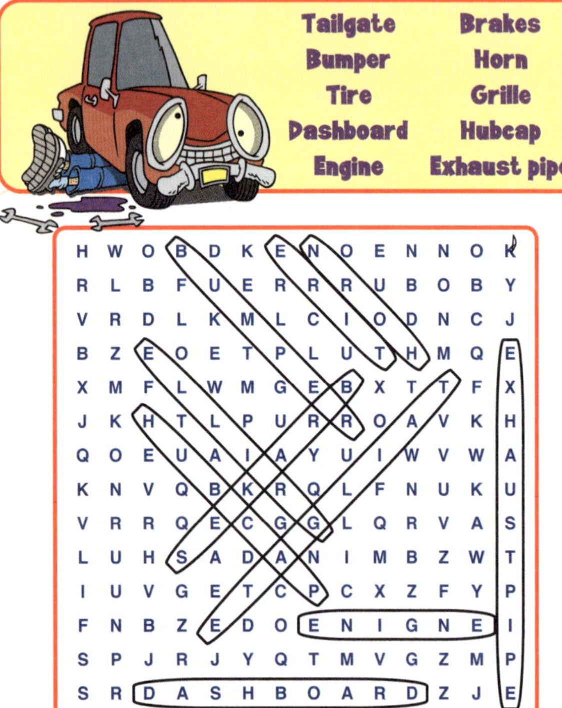

Page 101

Land the Plane

Page 102

Authors

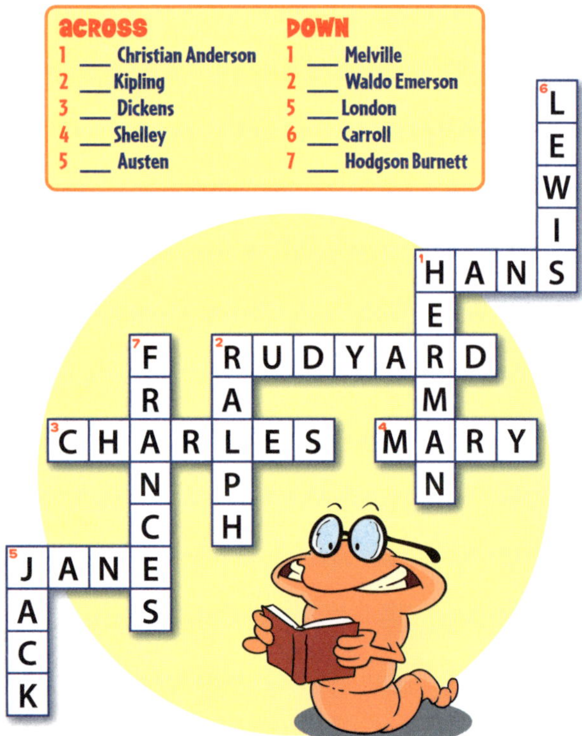

Page 103

Decode-a-Message

A=4	I=8	S=2
B=1	M=9	T=5
E=6	O=3	Y=7

B A B Y
1 4 1 7

B O T T O M S
1 3 5 5 3 9 2

Answers

Page 104
Double Aliens

Page 105
Influenza

INFLUENZA

Here are just a few:

ail, alien, elf, fail, fan, fez, fie, file, fin, final, finale, fine, flan, flea, flu, fuel, fun, funnel, inn, lane, leaf, lean, lie, lieu, life, line, linen, nail, nil, nine, nun, zeal

Page 106
Shopping Time

Page 107
I'm Hungry

Answers

Page 108
Dangerous Weather

– C – R + O + –

GON + R + 9 0 – ETY + G

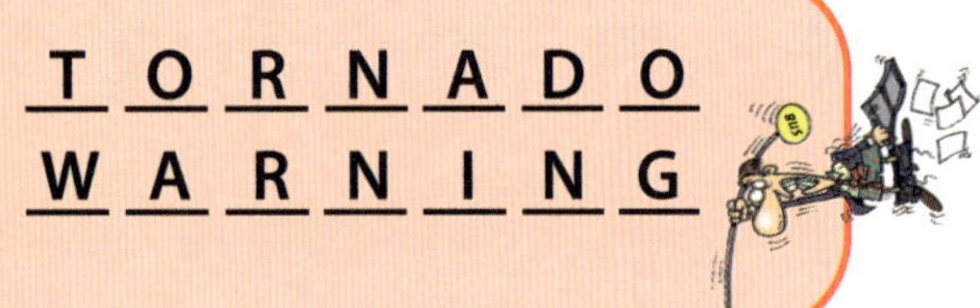

Page 109
Class Schedule

ACROSS
1 Latitude/ Longitude
2 Expressionism
3 Pythagorean Theorem

DOWN
4 Sonnet
5 War of 1812
6 Empirical Charts

		1 G	4 E	O	G	R	A	P	5 H	Y
			N						I	
			G						S	
6 C			L				2 A	R	T	
H			I						O	
E			S						R	
3 M	A	T	H						Y	
I										
S										
T										
R										
Y										

Page 110
Beach Time

Page 111
Sudoku

7	4	1	9	8	2	3	6	5
5	9	6	4	3	1	7	2	8
8	3	2	5	7	6	9	4	1
3	6	5	8	4	9	1	7	2
1	8	9	7	2	5	6	3	4
4	2	7	6	1	3	8	5	9
9	5	4	3	6	8	2	1	7
2	7	3	1	9	4	5	8	6
6	1	8	2	5	7	4	9	3

Answers

Page 112

Dino Paradise

Page 113

Word Scramble

(Bird of peace)

D O V E

HWOS

(Performance)

S H O W

HCSOK

(Surprise, stun)

S H O C K

LADE

(Hand out cards)

D E A L

KACP

(Put into a suitcase)

P A C K

KRWO

(Do a job)

W O R K

PLIF

(Turn over)

F L I P

IJNO

(Become part of a club or team)

J O I N

Page 114

Types of Birds

Mockingbird	Wren
Heron	Sparrow
Hummingbird	Woodpecker
Shorebird	Warbler
Bluebird	Duck

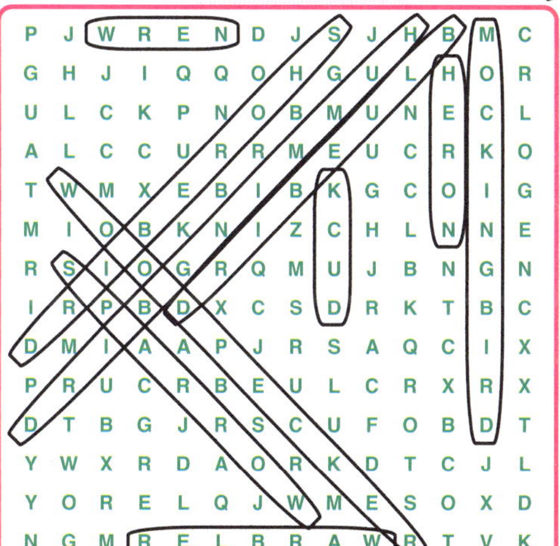

Page 115

Militaristic

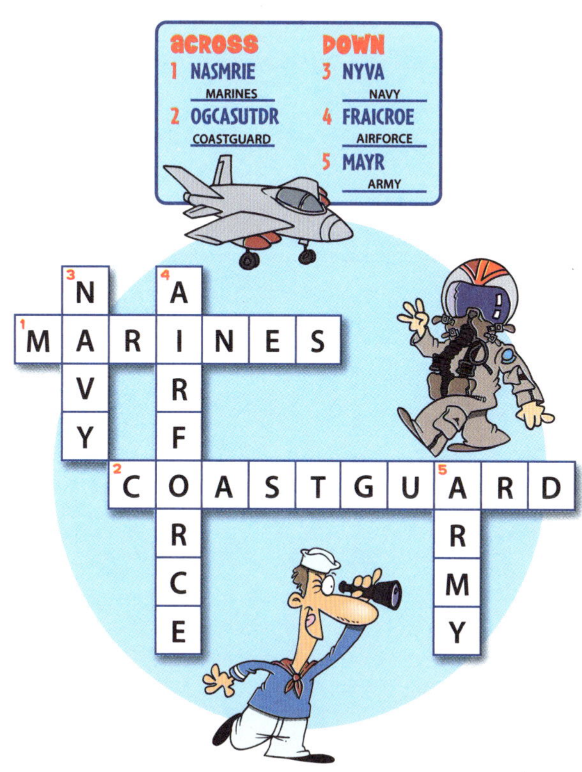

Answers

Page 116

Musical Instruments

ACROSS

4 Long, silver woodwind instrument

5 Woodwind instrument that sounds like a duck

6 Jazz instrument with a double reed

DOWN

1 Biggest baritone brass instrument

2 Second largest, upright orchestra instrument

3 Highest pitched band instrument

Page 117

Decode-a-Message

A=2	G=1	M=3	O=6	T=5
D=7	H=4	N=10	R=11	W=9
E=12	I=8			Y=13

H	A	I	R		T	O	D	A	Y
4	2	8	11		5	6	7	2	13

G	O	N	E
1	6	10	12

T	O	M	O	R	R	O	W
5	6	3	6	11	11	6	9

HAIR TODAY, GONE TOMORROW.

Page 118

Double Skydiver

Page 119

Veterinarian

VETERINARIAN

Here are just a few:

air	even	nerve	river
ant	event	net	tan
art	ever	never	tea
ate	inn	nine	tear
avert	inner	ran	tee
ear	invent	rant	ten
eat	invert	rare	tiara
enter	invite	rat	train
entire	irate	rate	trivia
era	near	rear	vain
eve	neat	rent	vine

Answers

Page 120
Even Plane Maze

Page 121
What Time Is It?

Page 122
Fun For All

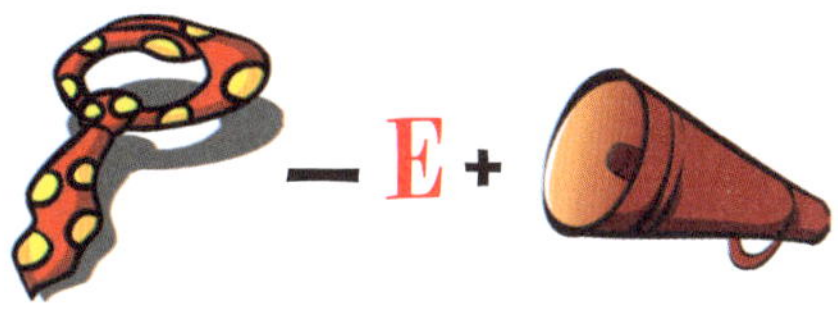

– GA – PHONE

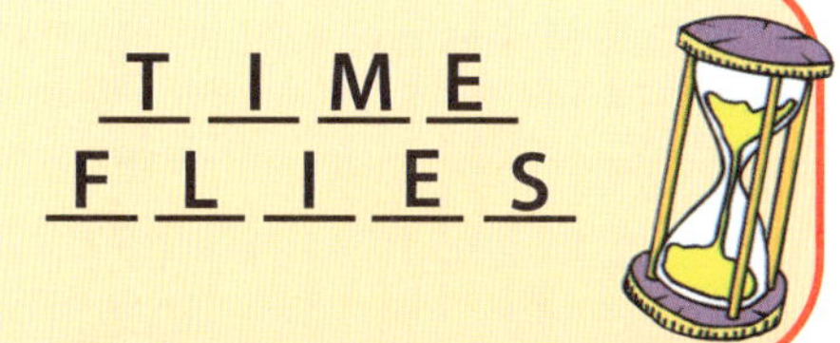

Page 123
Double Apples

Answers

Page 124
Pretty Peacocks

Page 125

Page 126
Pyramids

Page 127
Word Scramble

VAERBEEG
(Thirst quencher)
B E V E R A G E

REOEIHN
(Female hero)
H E R O I N E

YSYSEDO
(Epic journey)
O D Y S S E Y

BHRMAUEGR
(Goes with fries)
H A M B U R G E R

GIISHATNKGVN
(Holiday)
T H A N K S G I V I N G

OEOTCSINRNVA
(Long chat)
C O N V E R S A T I O N

ELADTOR
(Ballerina wear)
L E O T A R D

OGBIWLN
(Rolling game)
B O W L I N G

Answers

Page 128

Healthy Food

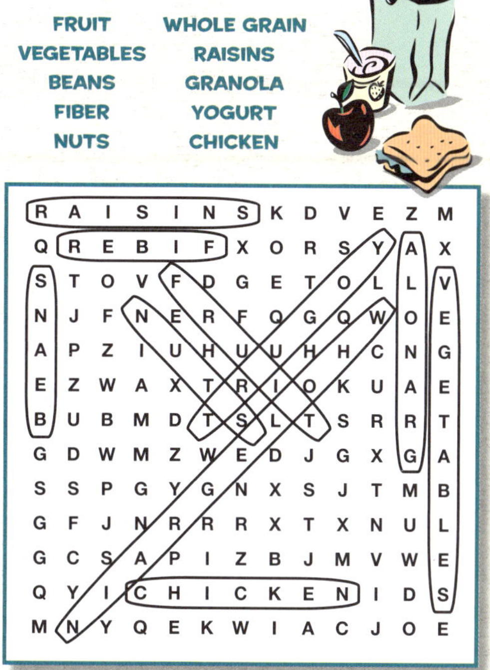

Page 129

Sudoku

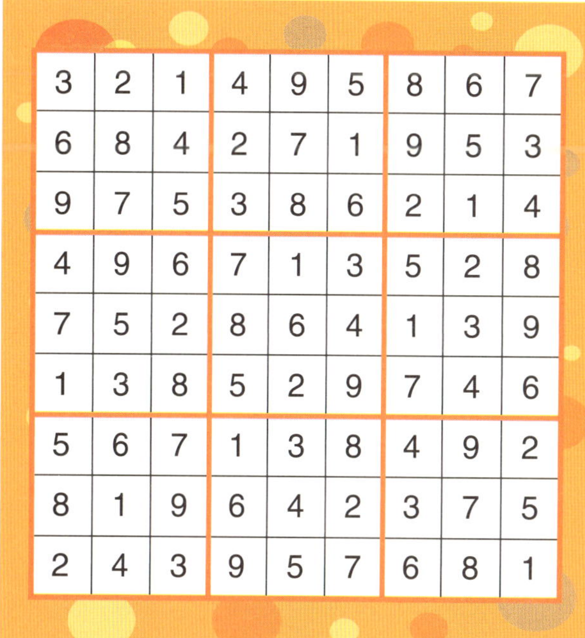

Page 130

Building a House

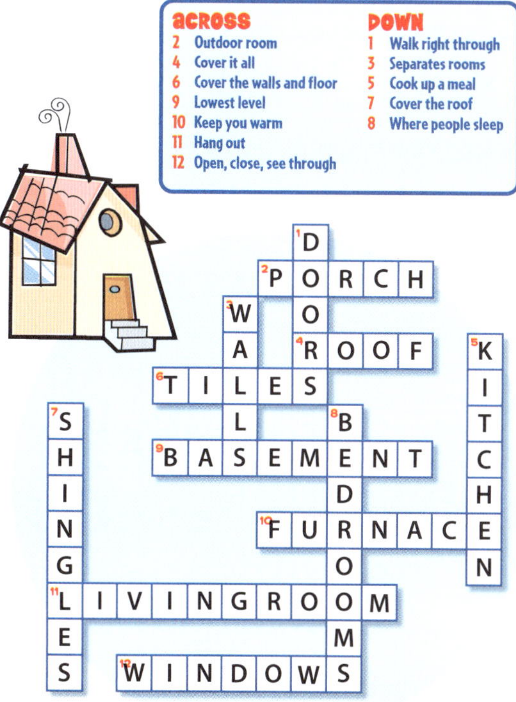

Page 131

Decode-a-Riddle

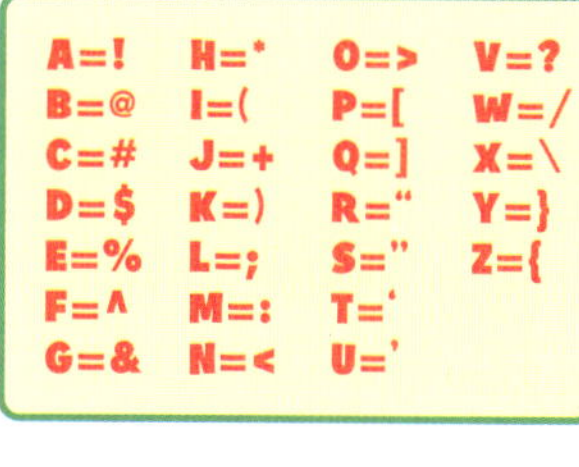

WHAT IS AN ORANGUTAN'S FAVORITE TOOL?

A MONKEY WRENCH

Answers

Page 132
Animal Habitat

Page 133
Dinnertime

DINNERTIME

Here are just a few:

deem	ere	nine	tie
deer	indent	red	tier
den	item	rent	time
denim	mend	ride	timer
dent	mere	rind	timid
die	merit	rite	tin
dim	met	tee	tire
dime	meter	ten	tired
dine	mite	tend	tree
dinner	nerd	tender	trend
enter	net	term	tried

Page 134
Get to Class on Time

Page 135
In the Cupboard

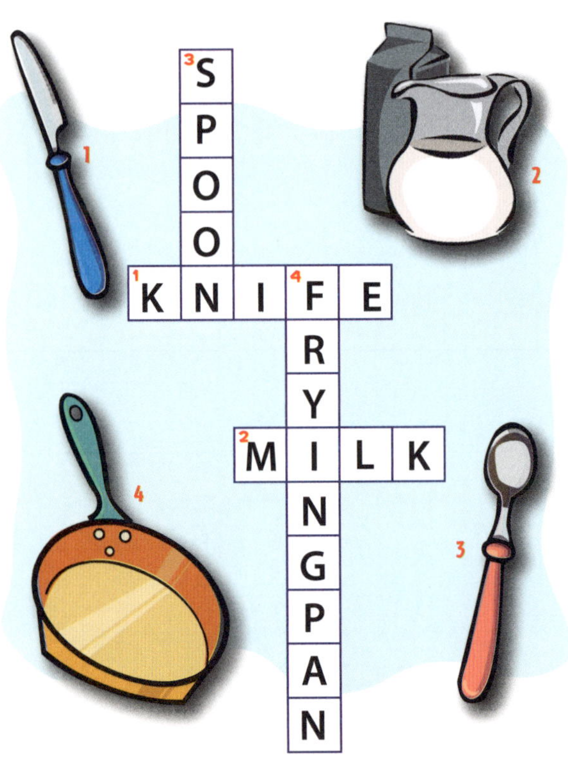

Answers

Page 136

Name of a Leader

Page 137

School Bus

Page 138

Track and Field

Running
Hurdle
Start
Finish
Crossbar
Endurance
Relay
Interval
Spikes
Training

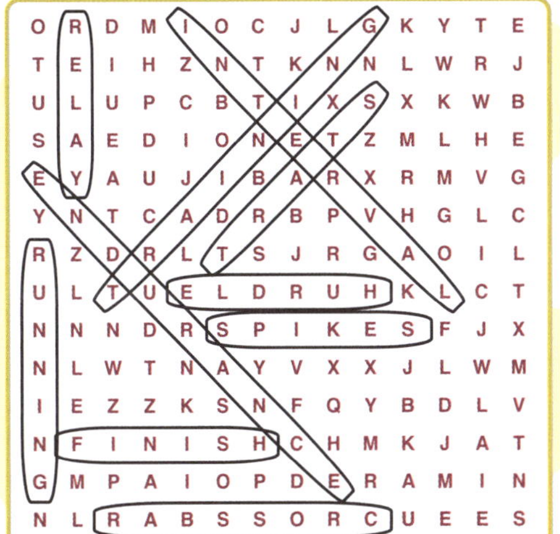

Page 139

More State Capitals

Answers

Page 140

Lemonade Stand

Page 141

Word Scramble

SOGOE
(Bird)
G O O S E

YDINW
(Air moving)
W I N D Y

TRAGUI
(Instrument)
G U I T A R

JNUAC
(Spicy style)
C A J U N

BITRBA
(Twitchy animal)
R A B B I T

EHUSO
(Dwelling)
H O U S E

Page 142

Classic Books

Page 143

Sudoku

8	4	2	9	5	3	6	1	7
7	1	9	2	8	6	5	3	4
6	5	3	7	1	4	9	8	2
3	8	1	5	7	2	4	9	6
2	6	4	3	9	8	7	5	1
9	7	5	6	4	1	3	2	8
1	9	6	4	2	5	8	7	3
4	2	7	8	3	9	1	6	5
5	3	8	1	6	7	2	4	9

Answers

Page 144

Time To Laugh

Page 145

Decode-a-Message

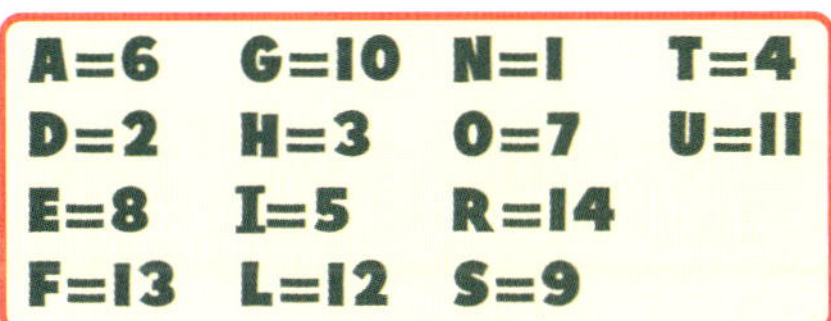

THERE IS A LIGHT AT THE END OF THE TUNNEL.

(4 3 8 14 8 / 5 9 / 6 / 12 5 10 3 4 / 6 4 / 4 3 8 / 8 1 2 / 7 13 / 4 3 8 / 4 11 1 1 8 12)

Page 146

Double Cats

Page 147

Alphabet Soup

ALPHABET SOUP

Here are just a few:

able	bet	hut	pale
about	blast	lab	paste
alas	bloat	last	pat
aloe	blue	lash	path
also	boast	leash	pause
ape	halo	let	petal
ate	hate	lost	plate
bate	help	lush	plus
bash	hole	oat	salt
bath	hose	oath	sea
beast	host	out	seat

Answers

Page 148
Lucky Number 18

Start

18	12	13	17	13
18	12	12	15	15
18	18	12	14	13
17	18	18	17	19
14	15	18	12	17
19	13	18	18	18

Finish

Page 149
Sudoku

3	2	4	1
1	4	2	3
2	1	3	4
4	3	1	2

Page 150
Small Pet

Page 151
Scientific

SCIENTIFIC

Here are just a few:

cent	ice	nice	since
cite	infect	nit	sit
cities	infest	nite	site
fin	insect	scenic	ten
fine	inset	scent	tic
finest	its	sect	tie
fist	nest	sent	tin
fit	net	sin	

Answers

Page 152

A Pirate's Life

Page 153

Page 154

Funny Farm

Page 155

Library Number

Answers

Page 156
Ocean Wildlife

Page 157
Multiplication Tables

Page 158
Read All About It

Page 159
Decode-a-Riddle

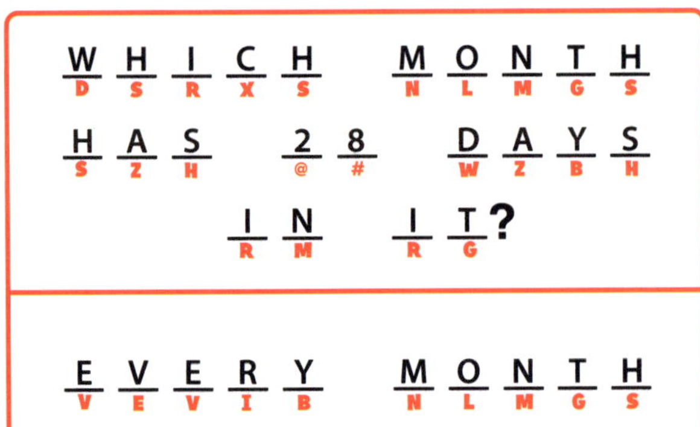

Answers

Page 160

Double Gumballs

Page 161

Rattlesnake

RATTLESNAKE

Here are just a few:

alas, alert, alter, ankle, area, ark, art, ask, eat, earn, ease

easel, eternal, kate, karate, knee, kettle, knelt, lark, laser, latter, learn

lease, nasal, near, neat, nest, rake, rank, rant, rate, rattle, reel

reek, rest, salt, sank, sea, sear, sleek, snare, state, take, treat

Page 162

Alien Odd Maze

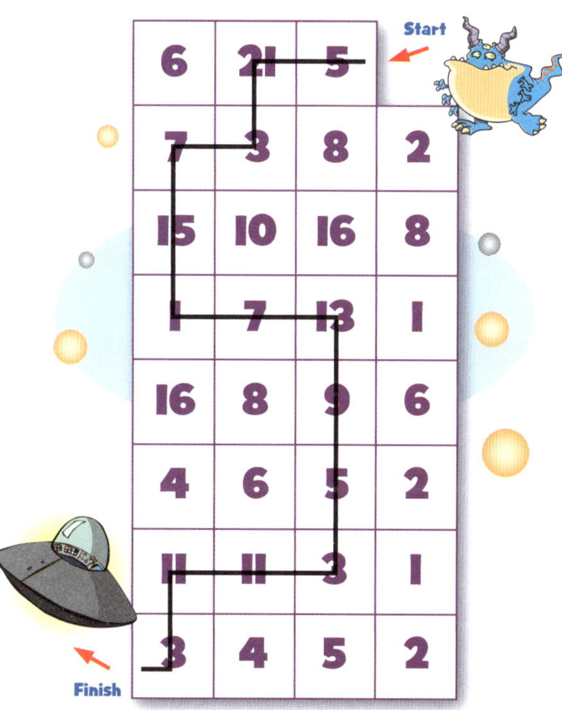

Page 163

Post Office

Answers

Page 164
Type of Book

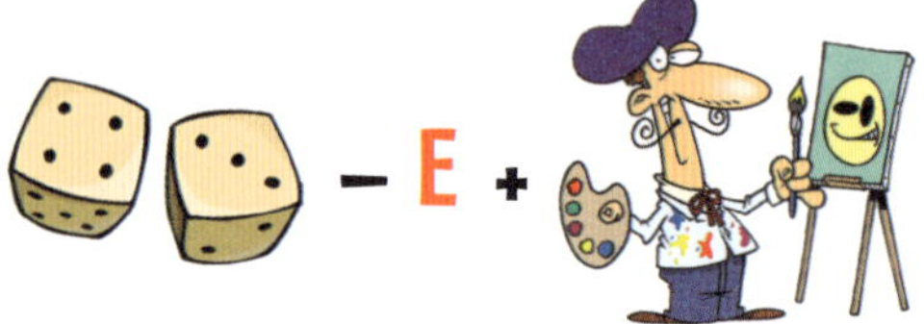

– AR – ST +

Page 165
Farm Animals

PIG	COW
HORSE	GOAT
SHEEP	DUCK
ROOSTER	GEESE
CHICKEN	DOG

M	F	Z	E	K	Z	U	J	G	M	W	O	B
E	J	M	C	Y	C	H	I	C	K	E	N	Z
O	Q	U	C	N	X	N	R	Q	I	A	V	T
Z	D	S	Y	C	J	U	O	L	F	K	V	K
K	A	Y	S	V	Y	P	O	X	T	K	D	E
G	B	R	T	B	H	U	S	W	R	H	Q	D
J	D	D	B	J	J	W	T	Q	E	Y	R	S
S	Y	O	V	K	O	X	E	G	Z	W	Z	H
H	T	U	G	C	W	N	R	J	F	C	E	O
E	J	G	H	Y	R	S	C	P	R	P	S	R
E	G	O	O	E	O	Y	Q	U	I	L	E	S
P	O	A	C	U	X	Q	V	G	W	L	E	E
K	R	T	U	E	F	E	A	J	W	N	G	Z

Page 166
Sudoku

4	2	9	7	8	1	6	5	3
5	1	7	3	4	6	2	9	8
8	3	6	9	2	5	7	4	1
9	7	2	5	1	3	8	6	4
1	8	4	6	9	2	5	3	7
6	5	3	8	7	4	9	1	2
2	9	1	4	6	8	3	7	5
7	4	5	2	3	9	1	8	6
3	6	8	1	5	7	4	2	9

Page 167
Double Builders

Answers

Page 168
Hockey Rink

Page 169
Word Scramble

WRAD
(Create a picture)
D R A W

ESMRG
(They cause sickness)
G E R M S

ETEHT
(They are in your mouth)
T E E T H

NISGW
(Go back and forth)
S W I N G

KAFE
(Not real)
F A K E

LMKI
(Drink it with cookies)
M I L K

PALEP
(Round, red fruit)
A P P L E

DOCL
(Chilly, freezing)
C O L D

Page 170
Jungle Animals

Page 171
Sudoku

8	3	1	7	6	4	2	9	5
7	9	6	2	5	8	1	3	4
4	2	5	1	3	9	6	7	8
3	4	9	8	2	5	7	6	1
6	8	7	3	9	1	4	5	2
1	5	2	4	7	6	3	8	9
5	1	4	6	8	7	9	2	3
9	7	3	5	1	2	8	4	6
2	6	8	9	4	3	5	1	7

Answers

Page 172

Autumn

ACROSS
1 The air gets ___ .
4 There is less and less _____ .
5 The trees get ___ .
6 Brightly colored leaves
7 Orange vegetables that can be carved
8 Put away light jackets, put on ______
10 Gathering of crops
11 The season to prepare for _____

DOWN
2 What falls in autumn
3 Light up the ____ .
6 Another name for autumn
9 Can harm delicate plants

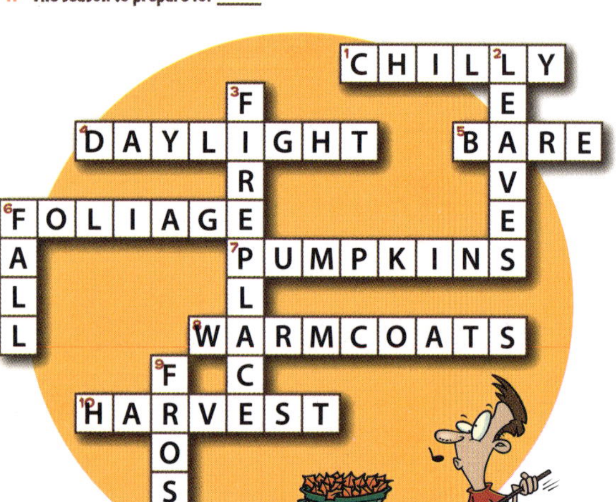

Page 173

Decode-a-Message

1=A	8=H	15=O	22=V
2=B	9=I	16=P	23=W
3=C	10=J	17=Q	24=X
4=D	11=K	18=R	25=Y
5=E	12=L	19=S	26=Z
6=F	13=M	20=T	
7=G	14=N	21=U	

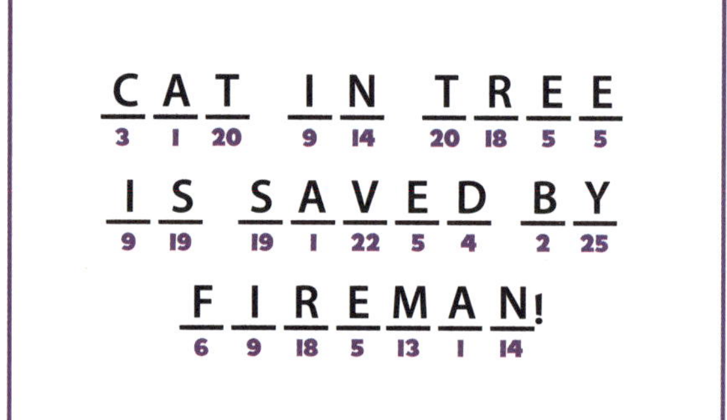

Page 174

Double Jack-o'-lanterns

Page 175

Scatterbrain

SCATTERBRAIN

Here are just a few:

ace	bent	neat	saber
acne	bitter	nest	scab
air	cabin	net	scar
arena	can	race	since
art	case	rain	stab
attic	eat	raise	state
ban	ice	rant	tact
bane	insect	react	tar
bare	insert	rear	tart
batter	intact	rib	tent
beat	near	rice	tribe

Answers

Page 176

Even Maze

Page 177

Types of Vegetables

Page 178

Family

Page 179

Sudoku

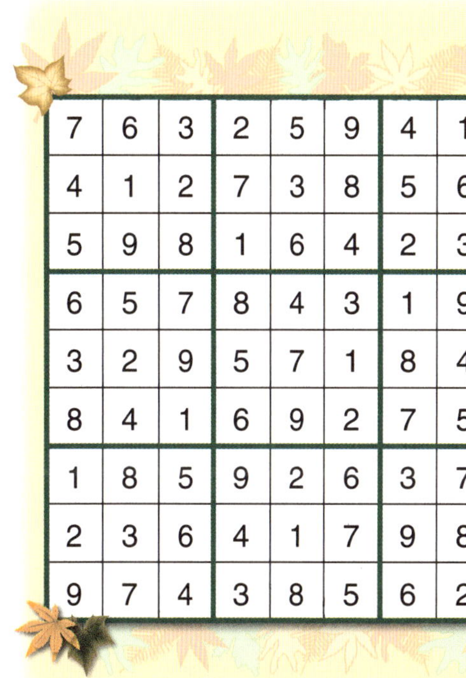

7	6	3	2	5	9	4	1	8
4	1	2	7	3	8	5	6	9
5	9	8	1	6	4	2	3	7
6	5	7	8	4	3	1	9	2
3	2	9	5	7	1	8	4	6
8	4	1	6	9	2	7	5	3
1	8	5	9	2	6	3	7	4
2	3	6	4	1	7	9	8	5
9	7	4	3	8	5	6	2	1